MINIATURE LIVING BONSAI LANDSCAPES

MINIATURE LIVING BONSAI LANDSCAPES

The Art of Saikei

HERB L. GUSTAFSON

Sterling Publishing Co., Inc. New York

Library of Congress Cataloging-in-Publication Data

Gustafson, Herb L.
  Miniature living bonsai landscapes : the art of saikei / Herb L.
Gustafson.
      p. cm.
  Includes bibliographical references (p.) and index.
  ISBN 0-8069-0734-7
  1. Saikei. I. Title.
  SB433.5.G875   1994
  635.9′772—dc20   94-13707
                                                    CIP

Book Design by Judy Morgan
Edited by R. P. Neumann

10 9 8 7 6 5 4 3 2 1

Published by Sterling Publishing Company, Inc.
387 Park Avenue South, New York, N.Y. 10016
© 1994 by Herb L. Gustafson
Distributed in Canada by Sterling Publishing
% Canadian Manda Group, P.O. Box 920, Station U
Toronto, Ontario, Canada M8Z 5P9
Distributed in Great Britain and Europe by Cassell PLC
Villiers House, 41/47 Strand, London WC2N 5JE, England
Distributed in Australia by Capricorn Link (Australia) Pty Ltd.
P.O. Box 6651, Baulkham Hills, Business Centre, NSW 2153, Australia
Printed in Hong Hong
All rights reserved

Sterling ISBN 0-8069-0734-7

Acknowledgments

The large size and complexity of some of the miniature bonsai landscapes made it necessary to switch from using my familiar 35-mm camera to medium-format equipment. Fortunately, I met Dick McRill, bird artist and photography expert. He painted the gorgeous blue sky backgrounds seen behind many of the landscapes. He helped me learn more about cameras and photography than I, perhaps, wanted to know. For you equipment buffs, the photos were taken under tungsten light with either a Zenza Bronica 6 × 6 or a Mamiya 6 × 4.5 with a 150-mm lens to minimize distortion. Thank you, Dick, for your patience with me.

Thanks go out to Bob Baltzer and Diane Lund for letting me photograph some of their nursery stock and saikei pots, respectively.

Kathy Hoy painted the beautiful Chinese brush paintings found throughout the book. I hope I can learn landscape painting from Prof. Hoy as well as she has learned bonsai from me.

Thank you, Branson Smith, for the use of your word processor, and, of course, many thanks to my wife, Susan, for the endless hours spent deciphering my handwriting in order to produce a manuscript. Thanks, Aleta and J.R., for your cooperation and accommodation while this book was being created. Special thanks go out to Wolfgang Amadeus Mozart for his "Requiem," for it was a strong motivator and constant reminder to me that I was on a deadline.

Contents

CONTENTS

Preface

I am a landscaper, both by education and by practical experience. As a student of landscape architecture, I did my share of toiling over balsa-wood models of buildings and arranging green plastic and spongy shrubbery just as the other students in those courses did. On the job site, the transformation of the miniature fake into a full-size reality seemed always to be an overwhelming task, yet one critical for the completion of the project. I admit that the design process itself was always the most fulfilling to me; that is why I wanted to be a landscape *architect*.

As part of my education, I was privileged to be a student at Toshio Kawamoto's Bonsai Saikei Institute in Tokyo. Each day I would take the subway to the Institute for the expressed purpose of creating landscapes in miniature. But, remarkably, those landscapes were alive! Miniature trees, carefully fashioned by the master himself, were available for use in assembling these living creations called *saikei*. Perfectly exquisite four- and five-inch-tall *crytomeria* had their delicate roots enclosed in tiny cloth bags just like the larger balled and burlapped nursery stock utilized in large-scale landscape projects. The same was true with his maples, elms, hornbeam, and cherry. Real stones became "boulders" in the created container garden. The soil was not just for show, fastened down with white glue, but rather quite real, poured around the plantings from the palm of my hand, just as if it were from a front-end loader on the job site. Perhaps you can imagine my excitement. A process of design and execution that used to take weeks was now only taking minutes. The creative process was alive and immediately gratifying.

That was twenty years ago. Since then I have used this art form to demonstrate to prospective clients what their gardens would look like when finished. I have been able to represent portions of large projects to boards of directors before commencing commercial work. These miniature landscapes communicate far more than blueprints, balsa wood, or plastic trees can. The clients have been universally enthusiastic and somewhat amazed. If additional documentation is necessary, accompanying blueprints can always be produced and a simple series of color photographs can be taken, copied, stored, or faxed. The ideas can be readily communicated to subcontractors on the job site.

Perhaps the best advantage of all, though, has been that this art form gives me the opportunity to create, disassemble, create again, experiment, and otherwise learn more about myself—and landscaping in general—in the privacy of my own home. I can successfully complete whole landscapes in an hour or so—in miniature. An added benefit, of course, is that a beautiful miniature landscape can be preserved for decades; simply water it as it starts to grow!

Creating miniature landscapes can be a very satisfying endeavor. As an art form this is saikei. Perhaps you will appreciate and understand this distinction if I differentiate the related art forms one by one.

Bonsai are miniature trees or plants that are kept confined by their container. With judicious pruning, these living art works can be maintained for centuries. Bonsai is by far the most popular and well known of all the miniature art forms, but there are several closely related creative activities.

Saikei is the art of creating the miniature living landscape. It utilizes living trees and combines them with rocks, soil, water, and related vegetation such as ground covers. The planting is done to scale as much as possible. Increased depth of view is created with optical illusions just as one might construct a stage setting or miniature diorama.

Bonseki is a bonsai-related art that creates landscapes in miniature, but without the use of living trees. In this book, as we learn how to sculpt the soil and arrange stones, we are actually creative "primitive" bonseki.

Bonkei, literally translated from the Japanese, is "tray landscape." Tradition allows the use of such items as clay figurines, lanterns, thatched huts, wooden bridges, boats, and the like. Many bonkei are formed from artificial substances such as papier-mâché and fibreglass.

The result is a landscape that might be comparable to the Western construction of a model railroad setting.

P'en Tsai is the Chinese equivalent of bonsai. Indeed, the word *bonsai* most probably derives directly from the older Chinese word. They even sound quite alike when pronounced with their respective regional accents. *P'en Tsai* focuses on individually potted plantings rather than forests, groves, or associated plantings.

P'en Jing is most closely associated with Japanese saikei. Rocks and trees harmonize in their containers; deciduous and evergreen trees combine for added effect. Grasses, bulbs, and mosses are added to the planting below the focus tree in an attempt to describe to the viewer the surrounding landscape. The concept of depth is suggested, but not well developed.

Suiseki is the art of displaying a single important stone. Fancy wooden stands are custom made for these unique stones which may resemble distant mountains, plains, valleys, and cliffs. Prized stones might contain a strip of crystal or quartz that evokes a waterfall, stream, or the ocean shore. Some look like thatched huts, seated buddhas, or animals, real or mythical. A special category of *suiseki* is reserved for stones that naturally exhibit the image of a chrysanthemum in full bloom, an age-old respect for the Emperor of Japan, who occupies the Chrysanthemum Throne.

These related art forms are each distinct; yet, at the same time, they share a common history, interest, and vision. I suspect that a miniature bonsai landscape has more appeal to makers of doll houses, movie sets, or model railroads than perhaps some other hobbies. I would encourage you to try it, however, regardless of your background or interest simply because it is easy, relaxing, and satisfying.

For those who have tried their skills at bonsai, I think you know what I mean when I say that it can be frustrating at times. Once the bonsai is styled and placed in the container, it feels as though times stands still. Further development of your bonsai goes at a snail's pace. If the trunk grows in diameter in one year, it seems so little as to be insignificant. The overwhelming feedback I get from advanced bonsai students is this: their frustration comes from the realization that a beautiful, old bonsai is something they may have to purchase. Waiting for their own creations to age and develop into masterpieces may not happen in their lifetime.

Saikei offers a satisfying compromise. Immature plant material can be arranged tastefully into a landscape. As the plants grow and develop, they can be "promoted" to a bonsai pot. In terms of difficulty and expense, saikei is the easiest of all the bonsai-related art forms to accomplish satisfactorily with a minimum amount of time, effort, and knowledge. A handful of stones, a few maple seedlings, and a homemade container can provide hours of first-class enjoyment, creativity, and personal growth. I recommend it to everyone.

Herb L. Gustafson

1

INTRODUCTION
TO SAIKEI

TOSHIO KAWAMOTO

Attempting to write a meaningful book on living bonsai landscapes without mentioning Toshio Kawamoto, it seems to me, would be negligent. It would be like discussing the evolution of the light bulb without a word about Thomas Edison. Few people realize that Kawamoto invented the art form. Professor Kawamoto owns and operates the Nippon Bonsai Saikei Institute in Tokyo, a unique educational establishment in urban Japan. Born into an established bonsai family, he has strived to make the art affordable and accessible to all. He is a gifted and expressive teacher and, naturally, author of the first book on saikei. This book is only the second.

Twenty years ago, I had the opportunity to travel to Japan to study bonsai. Professor Kawamoto's Institute was the first and most-mentioned place to begin. Getting off the subway and walking the few blocks to the address only served to intensify my feelings for the place when at last it was located. The effect was startling. Here I was, in and among tall buildings at the edge of downtown Tokyo, looking through a narrow gate into a world of miniatures. On both sides of the pathway leading towards the building were masterpieces of saikei on high shelves. Medium-high shelves contained trays of plant material all meticulously pruned with their rootballs enclosed tightly by some coarse fabric and tied with raffia. A large selection of flat trays and bonsai pots were at the far end. Below these shelves were boxes containing all sorts of rocks, ranging in appearance from highly decorative to fairly plain; types of rock that I had never seen before. They were gnarled, almost grotesque, with chunks of dark and light seemingly melted together. Some were reddish and highly striated. Still others were as flat as pancakes.

I entered the building at the end of the path; I was even more surprised. A class was in session and sitting at a half-dozen stools were students working on projects. I recognized Professor Kawamoto working with one of his pupils. He had matured a bit from his book jacket photo that I remembered, but it was definitely he. I was offered help from a man who turned out to be Tom Yamamoto, Kawamoto's number-one sidekick and chief business associate. I was startled by his courtesy and clear English. About a month later, I complimented him on his diction, explaining how some difficult English words, including my own name, seemed effortless to him. He replied, "It should be pretty good. I'm an American." I apologized profusely, but he insisted that it was "no problem"; it was a common assumption that he was Japanese.

With Tom Yamamoto's help, I registered, got a brief tour, and scheduled my first classes. Of all my bonsai experience before and since then, nothing compares to the electricity and excitement of that first day in class. I was assigned a work station, and I went to sit on the stool. In front of me was a beautiful, yet functional, work surface complete with turntable and saikei tray with the drain holes properly prepared with screen secured by copper staples. Drawers to my right revealed pruning tools, wire cutters, miniature rakes, tiny brooms, root hooks, spatulas, and *jin*-making pliers. Below were bins full of all types and sizes of soil ingredients. Huge spools of solid copper wire to my left were mounted on spindles for easy access. Trays full of moistened plant material were also off to the left. I made a mental note to myself right on the spot: this is the way to teach bonsai! Eventually, I hope to be able to offer my students the same combination of facilities, equipment, tools, and other teaching aides as what Kawamoto had assembled for his.

For the next few months, all I did was compose and disassemble landscapes. A combination was critiqued by the master. He would usually alter or modify my attempt in some way to make it better. This was amazing in itself; it seemed no matter what I put together, the professor could come around and, with a few quick motions with his hands, improve the planting, and also explain to me why it was better. Imagine spending an eight-hour day alternately making and taking apart landscapes. By the time I had graduated from the Institute, I felt that I had a close personal relationship with every rock and every tree on the premises. But this is the way to learn, and I have nothing but the utmost respect for the master, his school, and his staff.

THE ART OF SAIKEI

I am often asked how it was possible to go to school in Japan without speaking Japanese. Anyone who has travelled to Japan will agree with me when I say that the Japanese are eager to learn English. I had polite citizens stop me on the sidewalk and ask me if I would mind speaking with them for a moment just so they could practice! Most of my classes in Japan were in English therefore, as a sort of exchange: English lessons for bonsai lessons. My teachers' needs and my needs were mutually satisfied.

Years later, in the summer of 1977, our local bonsai society hosted the annual International Bonsai Society convention in Portland, Oregon. Both Toshio Kawamoto and Tom Yamamoto were featured speakers, and I had a chance to be reunited with them for a few days. Their visit to my bonsai nursery during the convention was memorable. As we three passed along my shelves of bonsai and saikei, the quiet was unnerving until at last the master reached out to a small grove of pine trees. With no hesitation he startled me by tearing them apart and then rearranging them in the container. I quickly looked over at Tom Yamamoto, who seemed to be trying to contain a grin. The professor was explaining why the trees had to be moved around as his hands worked. Glancing around, he spotted a few stones lying on the ground, and incorporated them into the planting as well. About three minutes later, satisfied with the improvements, he repositioned the small grove of pine trees on the shelf, and we continued down the aisle.

Mr. Yamamoto explained later that Professor Kawamoto might not realize that his abrupt actions could be perceived as in any way insulting. I reassured him that I considered it a compliment always to be treated as one of his students. His impact on me has been great. I believe that it must be as meaningful to all the others who have passed through his Institute. Working at the next workstation to my right, years earlier, had been a gentleman named Masa Furukawa. To my left worked Deborah Koreshoff. They are both present-day masters in bonsai and saikei in their own right. The number of students over Kawamoto's lifetime who have been touched by his genius gives one pause. Without the professor, this project would not have been possible.

DEFINITION OF SAIKEI

Translating straight from the Japanese characters, one gets a rather abrupt, abbreviated idea about saikei. The "bon" in bonsai is a pot or container, and the "sai" is the tree or planting. The same "sai" begins the word saikei. Saikei, then, is a plant or planting of some kind. Bonkei is a related art form where rocks, sand, and gravel are assembled to resemble natural landscapes. The "bon" in bonkei is the same "bon" as in bonsai; a container.

Saikei literally translates as "planted landscape." In English, it would be more comfortably expressed transposed as a landscape planting. Just as the definition of *bonsai* does not refer to the size of the trees, neither does that of *saikei*. Whereas size limitations are not part of the definitions, they are a very real part of the practicality of each art form. A mountain setting, for example, would have very small trees as compared to the rocks. However, being able to move the finished work may preclude trees taller than four inches high! Saikei encourages the use of small, young, and developing trees. This contrasts with bonsai, which requires long periods of time, and encourages the development of trunk girth, branch design, and a *lack* of accessory items such as rocks or ground covers.

To my mind, saikei is designed perfectly to satisfy the creative urges of a naturalist. By using a few seedlings, a random handful of rocks, and some soil, gravel, and moss, a saikei creator can convincingly represent a range of landscapes including most of the perennial favorites. An apartment dweller can create a nice Japanese garden in a shallow tray and enjoy it on the coffee table or rear balcony. City dwellers can create a grove of maples on their kitchen windowsill. Similarly, a windswept canyon, impractical to construct in any full-sized garden, is easily accomplished in a saikei pot.

Miniature landscapes are simple creations designed to evoke the visual pleasure one gets in the wilderness. The scene could be a running stream, a gorge, the seacoast, or any other real or imagined landscape. Miniature landscapes are just part of many closely related bonsai art forms. Each of them is easy to define in words, but impractical to define in actual use. For example, does a bonsai become saikei if it is planted on a rock? There are rock-grown bonsai just as there are saikei plantings that contain only one tree and one rock. The grey areas between these definitions are numerous and varied. Based on my study and experience, I believe it would be unfair to bonsai art in general to restrict free movement between its closely related forms just because of some artificially imposed semantic definition.

A bonsai rock planting normally involves a single large stone that represents a mountaintop or cliff. The rock should explain the shape of the tree just as the tree should communicate to the viewer its position on the rock. Where a rock planting normally shows the close-up of this relationship, saikei demonstrates the bigger picture. It is almost as if a close-up photograph of a portion of a saikei could be called a rock planting. The miniature landscape supplies more information. Is the cliff overhanging a stream? Is the mountaintop part of an island? Additional cues are provided by ground covers: mosses, ferns, and shrubbery. Most likely, a complex rock planting with several trees, gravel, and ground cover would be considered saikei.

OTHER RELATED BONSAI ART FORMS

Bonkei are nonliving landscapes. Land contours are often fabricated out of papier-mâché or fibreglass resins and painted. Gravel is typically glued down to make the planting more durable. Trees and shrubs may be plastic, foam, sponge, cloth, or silk. Lakes can be made out of glass mirrors on which rest a miniature boat floating in transparent glue. The use of clay figurines, mud huts, and wooden bridges is common. The imagination, attention to detail, and optical illusion are essentially the same as required for saikei.

Bonseki are nonliving landscapes as well, but they specifically avoid such trappings as human figures, thatched houses, and boats. The landscapes are constructed entirely out of stones, gravel, sand, and soil. Special attention is given to land contours to help achieve an effective statement. In Chapter Six, on creating saikei, we assemble many landscapes by starting with the larger rocks, followed by a "skin" of topsoil. If we were to stop at this point and not add the living vegetation, we would have a bonseki. If we added silk trees at this point, we create bonkei. If, instead, we utilize living plants rather than artificial ones, we form saikei.

P'en Jing is a Chinese landscape. It may contain living trees or not. It may contain houses, mud figures, and bridges—or not. The important distinguishing characteristic that separates this art form from its Japanese counterparts is found in its spirit or intent. *P'en Jing* exists in the minds of its creators. It is not a reproduction or photographic image. Each portrays a mystical, wonderful land where one might want to go. Some plantings are made out of respect for the stone itself. The cliffs might be formed out of a particularly well formed coral. Islands might be made out of large chunks of charcoal or petrified wood. Prehistoric fossils embedded in sedimentary sandstone might suggest the perfect form of a mountaintop. Nevertheless, it is the spirit of the planting that is of the utmost importance. More impressionistic than still life, the *P'en Jing* moves one's emotions somehow. The cliffs are somehow more precarious, the rock ledges narrower, and the gorge walls more precipitous than in actual life. *P'en Jing* are larger than life, even in their "miniature" size; actual container size ranges between three and five feet in length. The narrow trays might be just a thin slab of marble or granite placed on a carved rosewood stand. The shiny surface of the pot is usually all that is needed to represent water. The stones rest on their own natural or cut bases. In saikei, capturing a moonlit, starry sky on distant mountain peaks might be comparable to a photograph by Ansel Adams or Ray Atkeson. A *P'en Jing* of the same scene might capture a spirit more like Van Gogh's *Starry Night*.

P'en Tsai is the Chinese equivalent of bonsai. Their literal translations are identical. I suspect that *bonsai* is derived from the Japanese pronunciation of *P'en Tsai* hundreds of years ago. The Chinese tend to utilize bolder colors in their containers, however. The earth

1-1

1-2

tones of the Japanese *Tokoname* ware pots (see **1–1**) give way to the brighter reds and golds reminiscent of Spanish or South American cultures (see **1–2**). Chinese containers are more likely to have calligraphy etched into the glaze; windowlike panels are often seen on the sides. The use of brighter glazes is a Chinese tradition. I don't even recall seeing a red or yellow glazed Japanese pot. Japanese red is a dull brick red and the yellow tends to be more ochre or pastel. Chinese reds and yellows are more like what you might see on new fire trucks and school buses.

Professor Leon Snyder, from Missouri, utilized miniature landscapes to help landscape architecture students learn about nature. A group of students would assemble rather large (six foot) living scale replicas of familiar places as a study project. Actual plant material was used wherever possible. These so called "micro-environments" turned out to be quite spectacular and detailed. To hear him talk of the initial site visit, its careful surveying followed by its meticulous recreation in the classroom, was quite impressive. It sounded as though his concerns paralleled many of those in designing saikei.

Some years ago I visited a beautiful home in northern California while touring bonsai nurseries in the area. Directly inside the formal foyer was an incredible sight: a large terrarium. This was no ordinary terrarium. It was roughly the size of a five-foot cube. The glass walls were elegantly etched and bevelled. Inside was a model of an ancient Mayan ruin, complete with fallen porticoes and statuary. Around the temple were tropical trees and vines: figs, banyans, palms, and ferns. Lush moss covered the forest floor and even miniature orchids hung from the tree trunks. The owner insisted that the planting only required about one cup of water once every summer. The rest of the moisture was simply recirculated inside the glass. The plants recycled their own oxygen and carbon dioxide. But is it saikei? Kawamoto probably would have thought "No," but would have liked it anyway.

If I were to try to establish some sort of hierarchy for all the bonsai-related art forms, I would place saikei as the first order of the ranking. It utilizes the youngest plant material, it is the least expensive, it develops quickly, and it requires little more than imagination. As plants mature and develop over the years, they may be removed from the saikei container and "promoted" to bonsai. By no means do I view this entry-level position as a criticism or as a derogatory remark. Those of you who are frustrated with the time and maintenance involved in bonsai will see saikei as a breath of fresh air in a hobby that can be quite stuffy at times. For the beginner, it is an excellent way to get your feet wet. In the saikei classes that I have taught, I have observed complete beginners—a flat tray in front of them with a pile of stones and some sand—dive into a project with zest, full of ideas and experimentation. The same beginners armed with a pruning tool in front of a potential bonsai pine tree will sit there motionless with fear and trepidation because they are afraid of making a mistake.

It may surprise the reader that no landscape in this book took more than two hours to create. Most were made in less than an hour, and then taken apart after being photographed. No problem, I can just make another one. Maybe the next one will be better! Try doing that with bonsai; it cannot be done. Once the branch is cut, the tree either looks better or it looks worse. You can't just say, "Oh well!", tear it apart and start over again. I hope you are beginning to see the advantages to saikei.

Bunjin style, historically speaking, belongs to the highest order in the bonsai hierarchy. Ancient Chinese philosophers, writers, and painters established the *bunjin* as the pinnacle of *"literati,"* or learned man, thinking. As the beginner progressed through amateur to advanced, master status was conferred on the most worthy. Art, literature, philosophy, ethics, and the personal style of the master were combined to create signature works of art. These could be works of poetry, drama, music, landscaping, essays, lectures—or bonsai. These signature pieces had the special designation of *bunjin*. It saddens me somewhat to see a beginner hack away at a sparse pine tree just to try to make it look *"bunjin."* In such a case the student has not made the connection between the lifetime of experience and understanding that allows the true master to go beyond ordinary categories to create the signature style termed *bunjin*.

By now I hope you have a good idea of what saikei is and how it relates to other bonsai art forms. With this brief overview complete for our purpose of developing a conceptual understanding of saikei, it is time to roll up our sleeves.

MATERIALS NEEDED

I continue with a brief description of pots, trays, containers, and slabs. Then I move on to rocks: what to look for and where to find them.

Containers

A brown *Tokoname* ware Japanese saikei tray is shown in **1–3**. This particular tray is the one most often used by the Nippon Bonsai Saikei Institute. It is a 24-inch by 19-inch oval. Its height is two inches, but appears to be much less, due to the way the outermost lip protrudes. This edge treatment makes the container an excellent choice for young plant material. Thicker and heavier pots harmonize best with thicker and heavier trees. Notice the large drain holes. They must be covered with hardware cloth or soffit screen and secured with copper wire staples or else saikei soil will readily fall through. The copper of the staples repels slugs, snails, sowbugs, or beetles, keeping them from entering the container from the underside of the pot. This earth brown color is especially suited to harmonize well with broadleaf evergreens and conifers, including the deciduous conifers such as bald cypress, larch, tamarix, Montezuma cypress, and dawn redwood. Brightly colored deciduous trees look best in a brightly glazed blue, green, or ivory container.

The thick blue stoneware container shown in **1–4** is from Japan. Its heaviness would complement a fairly mature grove of maples or elms. Five trees with trunks varying from one to two inches in diameter would balance the container's proportions. By including several fist-sized stones, the harmony would be further enhanced. This container is a 17-inch by 13-inch rectangle, 3½ inches high.

1-3

1-4

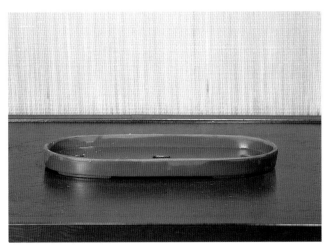

1-5

Narrow oval containers like the one shown in **1–5**, measuring 16 inches by 6 inches, do not lend themselves easily to miniature landscapes requiring a great deal of depth. This tray is more suitable for a windswept conifer, an extreme elongated style, or, perhaps, a slanting tree on top of an elongated stone. If you plant a pot like this with multiple trees, make sure they are not positioned all in a straight line from side to side.

The brown oval Japanese container shown in **1–6**, measuring 22 inches by 17 inches, 2½ inches high, is extremely useful. This type and size of tray complements all conifers with a trunk size exceeding one inch in diameter. It does particularly well with groves of young pine collected from woods.

Small containers such as those shown in **1–7** are ideal for first- and second-year seedlings and cuttings. Tiny

1-6

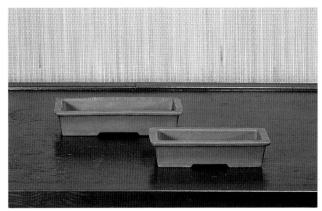

1-7

landscapes can be created in them in just a matter of minutes. As the trees develop over time, they can be transferred to larger trays or added to other existing miniature landscapes. One measures 7 inches by 3 inches, 1½ inches high; the other measures 8 inches by 4 inches, also 1½ inches high.

Even some traditional bonsai containers can be utilized for certain types of landscapes. A brown oval pot measuring 13 inches by 10 inches, 3 inches high, is shown in **1–8**. Normally the trunk size of the tree is so small in saikei that a three-inch-deep container would look too heavy by comparison. However, if we place a substantial stone in the planting (see **1–9**), we hardly notice the thick sides of the container. We now can plant a four-year-old pine tree on this rock ledge in a semi-cascade style, and we have formed a very nice landscape in a bonsai pot. A four-year-old pine alone in this big container would not work; but the rock adds sufficient mass so that the landscape will look balanced.

Containers can be made at home out of cement for those who are handy with concrete or other gypsum-related products. Temporary containers can be easily fabricated from wood or one of the cultured marble products on the market. Flat plastic trays originally designed to trap drainage from large outside planters can make an inexpensive alternative. Some people are comfortable working with fibreglass; still others have manufactured nice-looking containers out of compressed polyurethane foam. Perhaps you can think of other materials that have not been tried. I once saw an effective planting in a truck brake drum.

How about the rocks themselves as containers? Plant your trees in rock crevices, and just place the rock on a wooden stand. Who needs a pot at all? Flat stepping-stones make attractive bases for forest plantings. Moss holds the soil in place. Cupped rocks can create a hillside landscape sweeping from one side to the other. You can place rocks on top of rocks. A horizontal piece of slate can be the pot and a rock-grown landscape can be planted on top of it. Use your imagination. For a further extended discussion of growing containers, how to make a simple wooden landscape tray and other saikei trays, please see those sections found in Chapter Four.

1-8

1-9

Rocks

Rocks, stones, and gravel can be found in many places. When travelling, I like to keep a sharp eye out for potential sources. These include the mountains, local streams, commercial quarries, aquarium supply houses, rock and mineral shops, and nearby cliffs and outcroppings. However, the easiest and most available source tends to be masonry and landscape supply yards. Here you can find large bins full of decorative rock available by the pound. Some rocks are dumped between concrete dividers for landscape use. Still others are bound together with wire for use in fabricating chimneys, fireplaces, or similar masonry projects. These establishments offer the best source for most miniature landscape enthusiasts—especially for those who do not get out into the country often.

1-10

The pile of basalt shown in **1–10** was collected for the purpose of building rock walls, retaining walls, fancy fireplaces, and the like. From this pile, I found the rock for the *P'en Jing* planting in Chapter Six. Most landscape supply outlets are very tolerant when it comes to customers who want to pick through the piles. You can usually place your selections in a wheelbarrow provided, and when your selection is complete, drive it onto a scale that will weigh your newfound treasures. This is the easiest, least painful method to locate miniature landscape stones.

1-11

Lightweight pumice stones are shown in **1–11**. They can be hollowed out or shaped with a hammer and chisel to individual taste. I recommend this type of stone especially for individuals who might have difficulty with heavier types of rock. Large projects that involve a lot of stone benefit from this type of rock as well. Miniature landscapes should be designed to be portable. Do not make the mistake of assembling a "masterpiece" that cannot be moved. Admittedly, some landscapes might require four hands to move, but avoid creating something that requires a crane!

Large quartz rocks are shown in **1–12**. They can be used to make a desert scene, a snowcapped mountain scene, or a rock-grown landscape such as a Greek isle or the White Cliffs of Dover. They are expensive

1-12

and heavy; when you load your wheelbarrow, be conservative.

Limestone rocks such as those in **1–13** can be carved with an old hatchet or saw. They are not as heavy as quartz, but they can be just as bright in color. Sometimes fossil inclusions, or castings, can be revealed when they are broken apart—an added plus. If used for lush-type landscapes, they need to be coated with buttermilk before the planting is assembled. The alkaline nature of limestone rocks makes it impossible to grow moss on them without the acid of the buttermilk culture.

1-14

1-13

1-15

Lava stones can be found in yellow, red, brown, or black. Those shown in **1–14** are red stones from eastern Oregon. They have a sponge-like appearance to them. This even texture, however, makes them inferior candidates for scenes that require the illusion of depth. In order for the illusion to work, the front stones must display an increment size that differs with the rear stones (refer to Chapter Two). All forms of sponge-type lava have this drawback; however, they have some advantages as well. They can be carved to some degree and will absorb and retain moisture well. Lava rocks always have numerous nooks and crannies where plants can be secured.

Larger red lava rocks (see **1–15**) serve well as islands, volcanic mountains, or steep lava cliffs to which trees

1-16

can be fastened. They are the easiest to plant of any rock. Find a rock that looks like an island or a mountaintop, and plant trees on its spongy surface. If you need more room for roots, just cut away some rock with a chisel. If you need to support an overhanging tree, drive a nail into the rock and temporarily attach a string, wire, or net to the nail. This is something that is impossible to do with granite, basalt, or quartz.

Red lava cinders have two functions (see **1–16**). They can be screened to serve as bonsai soil (refer to Chapter Four), or they can look natural at the base of a miniature landscape that uses larger red lava rock. For example, if you composed an island scene out of a tall, imposing red lava rock with various tropical trees hanging onto its many cliffs and rocky ledges, a suitable shoreline could be made with red lava cinders. If you formed a mountaintop with a great red lava rock covered with moss and miniature trees, an appropriate scree could be made out of red lava cinders. Large rocks always decompose to smaller rocks with the passage of time. A granite cliff will always have decomposing granite at its base. A lava cliff will have lava cinders at its base as well.

The white sand shown in **1–17** is made of crushed quartz. It is manufactured to be applied to the tops of homes that have flat roofs which are sealed with roofing asphalt. While the tar is still sticky, a layer of this white crushed rock is applied to the flat roof. The gravel half

embeds itself into the still tacky surface and provides the homeowner with increased light and heat reflection that would be impossible without it. This manufactured gravel can be used as scree under miniature quartz mountains, or, after being screened, it can provide a whitewater effect in a stream landscape. Other white particles that work well are limestone fragments and packaged chicken grit from a livestock feed store.

The material shown in **1–18** is so-called beach rock. It could come from the beach or it could be scooped up from a stream bed. This is the type of rock that is most often used to represent water in full-sized landscapes. I admit, I have also used it on occasion for this purpose.

1-18

However, this example is really included here only to show what type of rock has absolutely no promise in forming a miniature bonsai landscape. I have seen a *P'en Jing* made of these rocks, but they were cut with a diamond saw and placed at odd angles. That was the exception to the rule. I cannot recommend using these rocks to create saikei.

Masonry sand is shown in **1–19**. It is formed especially to be combined with cement to mortar bricks together. Basically, it is man-made sand manufactured by crushing rocks. Its microscopic jagged edges are due to its origin from the mechanically crushed rock. These jagged corners serve to make a masonry mix that adheres

1-17

1-19

1-20

well to stone and brick for the construction of walls and foundations. Notice how the sand resembles rocky outlines as it is eroded by the rain. This type of sand is great for piling at the base of granite or basalt miniature cliffs for this reason. It naturally erodes just as decomposing granite would—as a scree at the foot of a thousand-foot-high cliff. Notice the pattern of erosion in the photograph of this sand. Doesn't it remind you of a distant arid hillside? You can use this effect on your miniature landscape by utilizing masonry sand instead of other natural sands.

Ordinary beach sand is shown in **1–20**. Its warm color will complement rich brown and gold rocks. It makes a convincing seacoast as well as a streambed. One note of caution: when using rocks, driftwood, or sand from the ocean, make sure that all salt and mineral residues are removed before use. Rinse thoroughly with fresh water for several days. For increased protection, add a bit of vinegar to the final rinse. Vinegar will remove latent calcium deposits that might still be salty.

Earlier in this section I mentioned how cooperative most retail landscape rock establishments can be with regard to bonsai and saikei enthusiasts. Masonry supply outlets can be a very good source of rocks as well, but some caution is advised. Often their stones are packaged for delivery to a job site rather than just lying in a pile. Be extra careful that you do not remove individual stones from preweighed packages of rock. State your

intentions at the front office beforehand and you will be guided to the areas where you can pick and choose.

Stacked and bundled stepping-stones are shown in **1–21**. They work well as layered landscape cliffs or as flat containers. Smaller specimens can function as vertical outcroppings.

Flat decorative stone facings such as those shown in **1–22** are usually used to cover broad surfaces of walls as a decoration. Laid down flat, they can make marvelous containers. Find a rock that has not been artificially cut with a saw. Some stones naturally fracture on beautiful curving lines and make an attractive base for a grove or forest planting. Try not to select a stone that is too long for its thickness. Remember, it has to be portable after planting. This type of thin rock comes in all shades of natural colors. Some have mica inclusions that sparkle; others have a wavy pattern of color. I have seen beautiful sea-green stone that works well as a seacoast landscape base.

Lava and other stone of volcanic origin such as welded tuff (see **1–23**) can appear somewhat spongy, but they can be nicely layered as well. Select rocks that are similar in color, striation, and thickness. Landscapes look best when all the stones look as though they are from the same geologic environment. Try to match, if possible, veins of color that streak through the rock. Two rocks can be made by breaking one rock in half with a hammer. Collect more rock than you think you will

1-21

1-22

1-23

need for your landscape. The extra rocks will give you more options while you design your miniature landscape.

Another rock source so often neglected can be found close to home in the form of natural or man-made outcrops. The small rock face shown in **1–24** is actually a quite natural columnar basalt outcrop. Elsewhere this feature has been given colorful names such as "the devil's post pile." Actually the post-like form is the result of cooling of the basalt millions of years ago. The molten basalt was injected between previous material and cooled slowly so that much later, when exposed at the surface, the rock fractures along planes of weakness that resemble three-dimensional mud cracks. Whatever their origin, rock climbers come to test their skills here and watch me curiously as I collect basalt stones from the scree at the base of the cliff to use in my miniature landscapes.

1-24

Plant Material

Generally speaking, most saikei material needs to be smaller, younger, and more delicately shaped than bonsai material. Bonsai has a broader range of appropriate plant material than does saikei. For example, *Ginkgo biloba*, a wonderful historic bonsai plant, in recent practice has only been considered borderline bonsai material because the leaves are somewhat large, the branches are too brittle for aggressive wiring, and the plant develops to maturity quite slowly. These considerations effectively eliminate the ginkgo for miniature landscape purposes. The smaller scale of the planting favors plant material that has small leaves, is easy to train, and matures quickly. For a complete list of suggested miniature landscape plant material, I refer you to the Plant Materials List under the Suggested Saikei Sources in the Appendices. For now, we can look at some of the characteristics that make some plants excellent candidates for saikei.

Japanese white birch seedlings are shown in **1–25.** There are approximately 50 two-year-old seedlings in this blue oval tray. The tallest is only eight inches in height. The leaves are in their late fall color with most of them already fallen after a frost. In spring, they will again shoot out with their new green leaves. Next year, the trunks will start to turn bright white.

1-25

1-26

1-27

1-28

Chinese elm is shown in **1–26**. This versatile plant has many varieties, including the *Seiju* elm, cork bark elm, *Hokkaido* elm, and the variegated elm. This plant is one year old from seed. As you can see, it is already acceptable for use in a miniature landscape.

There are a number of pine trees that are suitable for saikei. The pine shown in **1–27** is a two-year-old seedling of *Pinus mugho mughus*. Other forms—the Swiss mountain pine—Japanese black pine, Japanese white pine, have smaller internodes and shorter needles. The "*Yatsabusa*" designation of any plant simply means extremely dwarfed, thus *Pinus thunbergiana* 'Yatsabusa' would make excellent saikei material.

Pines grown from seed display a natural variation among their seedlings. The two Scotch pines, *Pinus sylvestrus*, shown in **1–28** came from the same cone. They are both the same age, yet the long-green-needled specimen will be unsuitable for bonsai or saikei purposes. Its siblings on the left displays short internodes, compact growth, and a wonderful steel-blue color, making it a prime candidate for a miniature landscape.

Cactus make wonderful miniature desert landscapes. Some types of cactus, such as those shown in **1–29**, look like miniature versions of larger cactus. Select cactus for its appearance and scale. Some *Euphorbia*, when they are young, grow with a small caliper, and the plant looks older than its actual age. Others begin their life as a large stumpy growth that will eventually elongate into its mature proportions. This latter type is not suitable as miniature desert landscape material.

An excellent two-year-old trident maple seedling is shown in **1–30**. Its leaves are small, the branches compact. This plant would make a marvelous saikei, especially planted over a rock. At this age, the roots would clasp tightly to the rock crevices, and, in just two more years, would start to look spectacular. As a bonsai, it would have to be field-grown for about five more years in order to thicken the trunk.

1-30

1-31

The two-year-old Japanese maple shown in **1–31** is a rare find. From among hundreds of seedlings of *Acer palmatum*, this one appears to be producing green and red deeply cut leaves that resemble the laceleaf Japanese maple. This tree will make superior saikei material. It already has an interesting trunk, beautiful foliage, and short internodes. Perhaps its greatest asset,

1-29

however, is that it is a laceleaf maple without the usual ugly graft mark.

Another excellent example of the natural variation found in plants is shown in **1–32**. These two *Zelkova serrata* grew from seed from the same parent tree. The plant on the right will make a good full-sized landscaping tree; it has already been pruned once. Its leaves are long and green, and the stem is straight and strong. The *Zelkova* on the left is exactly the same age. It produces an orange-copper-colored leaf all year long. The internodes are short and the leaf size is quite small. Notice also how the leaf tends to weep downwards as compared to the *Zelkova* on the right. This naturally dwarfed tree will make excellent saikei material.

The *Shimpaku* juniper is a favorite saikei plant. The four-year-old plant shown in **1–33** on the left had all the tips of its branches cut off last spring. In the container on the right is one of those tips which has rooted itself.

1-32

1-33

This juniper can be successfully air-layered as well. Notice that the younger and smaller plant on the right resembles a large conifer viewed from a distance. This optical illusion makes the *Shimpaku* an ideal plant for use in a miniature landscape.

Other trees that work particularly well are the *Tansu cryptomeria*, Waconda spruce, Little Gem spruce, *Yatsabusa* juniper, Skyrocket juniper, dwarf *arborvitae*, and Pixy pine.

SIZE CONSIDERATIONS

The illusion and scale of the plant is more important than the species itself. Select individual plants for their dwarf characteristics and avoid using fast-growing varieties. *Chamaecyparis thyoides* grows too fast. *Chamaecyparis thyoides andelyensis* is a better choice because it is more compact and is a slower grower. *Chamaecyparis thyoides andelyensis* 'Conica' is an even better choice for saikei, because it tends to grow in a cone shape just like a mature fir or spruce would in the wilderness.

Peruse nursery catalogs for suggested miniature trees. Most nurserymen are quite aware of the recent trend in popularity of bonsai-related activities and will indicate those plants that tend to work well. When shopping at a local nursery, select plants that look like miniature versions of larger, more mature plants. For example, thyme looks like a miniature version of sage. *Potentilla*, when it is not blooming, resembles a miniature scrub oak. Kingsbury boxwood looks like a tiny camellia, and so on. Design your landscapes in advance and consider what types and sizes of plants will be necessary to complete the illusion.

I find it helpful to sketch out the rough outline of a design on paper. The drawing should not be a work of art, it should just represent the scale of the rocks, plants, and container fairly accurately. I then can shop for appropriate-sized materials.

For example, the crude sketch shown in **1–34** represents a saikei idea. The drawing took about a minute to produce, but it solidified, on paper, the idea of the scale and proportion between the rocks, trees, and container. By using a tape measure on the paper, I now know that I will need one five-inch rock and two two-inch rocks. The trees will be five, four, and three inches tall and I will need an 18-inch brown oval tray with no drain holes in it so that I can add water to surround my "islands."

Now it is easy for me to rummage through my rock pile, shop for three appropriate-sized pine trees, and select the right container. Unless you have a large selection of saikei trays sitting around at home, this is a more accurate and predictable way to select just the right size container before the planting commences.

Always consider the weight of your completed planting. The above landscape design will weigh about twelve pounds when finished but without the water. The desert landscape discussed in detail later in Chapter Six weighed sixty-eight pounds. I have made four-hundred-pound landscapes. It all depends on the strength of you and five of your friends. As the seasons go through their cycles, you will probably want to relocate your landscape. It is a rare garden location that is ideal year round. An ideal summer location can be too dark and damp in the spring. A garden spot that offers nice winter protection may not be very nice for the fall display of colors. You might want to take your landscape to a local show sometime. You may have to, heaven forbid, move to another home!

1-34

To keep the initial expense down, I would recommend building a wooden pot as a training container. They are easy to assemble from plywood and prefabricated wooden mouldings for the edge. In a couple of years, your saikei will be developing quite nicely—or it will have died—but your starting investment will not have been cumbersome in any case. A successful planting can be promoted to a ceramic container at any time. Usually the roots of the trees grab hold of the rocks around them, and the transfer takes only seconds and can be accomplished at any time of the year.

It always seems to surprise bonsai and saikei beginners that the smaller the container, the more difficult the planting is to keep alive. Most often I hear the words "I'm just starting, so I want to begin with just a small planting." These people are starting at the most difficult end. Small bonsai and saikei will dry out in two hours in the summer. They will readily freeze in the winter. It is more difficult to achieve a sense of proportion and scale in a small container. For the beginner, therefore, I recommend a minimum of fourteen inches by nine inches with a depth of two inches for the starting container. If weight is a consideration, I recommend light lava, pumice, or feather rock to keep the planting portable by one person.

Remember that there are indoor plants, outdoor plants, and everything in between. Do not try to change the biology of the plant to suit your display needs. If you want a landscape in your kitchen window, simply select the appropriate plant material. You cannot grow a pine tree on top of your coffee table any more than you can grow florist azaleas in your garden, and yet, these are both tried continually. Within certain parameters, light can be increased in the house by skylights, bay windows, and grow lights to help you successfully grow plants inside. Conversely, shade cloths, screens, lattice, and ventilation fans may help you grow sensitive plants outdoors. Familiarize yourself with the plant materials available to you. Ask the florist or nursery staff that sell the plants where they can best be located. You may even want to construct a special stand or growing shelf where your planting can best be grown and admired.

With this brief overview of the art form of saikei, you are ready to start making sketches and planning your display shelves. Ask at local nurseries if a bonsai society meets in your area, and visit with some of the members. Ask questions, read other books, and maybe take a short class on bonsai or saikei if available. Visit bonsai nurseries, subscribe to a bonsai magazine. Especially, seek out those individuals who have tried making miniature landscapes. Learn from their mistakes. The more input and information you can surround yourself with, the greater your chances of enjoyment and success.

2

THE CONCEPT
OF DEPTH

ROCK BECOMES MOUNTAIN

I must have created an unusually poor saikei one day at the Nippon Bonsai Saikei Institute. Toshio Kawamoto himself, not one of his able assistants, had just torn my attempt all apart and was reassembling it rock by rock with generous doses of instruction. He picked up a rock and held it in his hand. "This way, the rock is just a rock," he stated. "Turn it on its side and it becomes a ledge." Placing his other palm against the rock and holding it over the tray, he said, "Now the same rock is the bank of a stream." And with the stone popping out of the top of both his hands, "Rock becomes mountain."

He smiled knowingly and nodding his reassurance to me, gestured towards the landscape in ruin and walked away. I didn't reassemble another landscape that day; I just sat and stared at the stones for a bit, and then called it a day. After several more days of building and destroying and building again, some degree of my confidence began to be restored.

LEVELS OF DEPTH, FOREGROUND, BACKGROUND

A little information about the perception of depth is helpful to the beginner. What makes an object appear near or faraway? What signals are the eyes receiving that establish depth? What role do our two eyes play prior to signalling the brain about close versus distant objects?

The art of *suiseki* seems a bit odd to those who encounter it for the first time. A rock that resembles a distant mountain is placed on a custom-made elaborate wooden stand and displayed on a shelf. After having seen many *suiseki*, one naturally compares them, selects favorites, and rejects others that have less personal appeal. Almost without noticing, the viewer is drawn into the miniature world of representing rocks as mountains or distant hills, ravines, waterfalls, and valleys. Before long, you find yourself picking up rocks at the beach or in the mountains and looking at them in an entirely different way. The same process happens in saikei. Soon, the common bonsai grove just doesn't seem adequate any longer. You seek out new designs to attain more depth, arrange trees differently, look at the landscape with a broader perspective in mind. This is all part of the natural learning process. We start with a little knowledge, apply it to an experience, improve it, judge it against known standards, and then seek out more knowledge. The cycle repeats itself over and over again.

The full-sized Japanese garden is built around the assembly of viewing points along the garden path. Benches are provided as a not too subtle suggestion that a particular location is a good viewing point. The view that is presented will often have overhanging branches and nearby tree trunks to help frame the "picture" and provide the foreground focus. A middle-distance scene is established farther away, perhaps with a mounded maple tree or leaning pine over the water. More subtle, but always present, is the attention to the distant scene—an element that is not included in Western gardens. This distant scene provides the depth that puts the foreground and middle distance into their proper perspective. Without this depth, the viewer is basically looking at the simple bonsai grove again: "what you see is what you get." Without the depth, the scene is just average; it is not inviting. It is like entering a room which has no other exits, no windows for the eyes, and no doors to provide a passageway. You glance into such a room and do not feel particularly like entering. If you do enter, you do not feel like staying long.

If the eyes are allowed to escape into the next level of depth, the planting becomes inviting. It is like adding windows to the room or a corridor along the far wall. One is then tempted not only to enter the room, but also to linger in it awhile, look around, and pass to the other side, glancing through the windows occasionally. The garden becomes less enclosed, less stifling, and more inviting.

Good miniature landscapes take advantage of this

visual phenomenon. The use of close, middle, and distant focal points adds interest, and personal involvement for the viewer of the planting. Depth may be provided by the most subtle of elements. It might be provided by a curving path going "out of sight," a single distant tree, or a bubbling stream source just out of view. It does not have to be as obvious as a distant snow-capped peak. Just the idea that some of the back trees are hard to see is sometimes all that is needed. It draws viewers into the planting. Viewers will want to move towards the saikei, and adjust their eyes back and forth a bit to see the distant trees in the back of the planting.

I enjoy watching people looking at bonsai shows. Often an inexperienced eye is actually the best judge of a planting. If a saikei gets long stares from people who have their arms folded in front of them, it suggests to me that the planting might be basically boring and that the viewers may be trying to figure it out—asking themselves just why it is on exhibit. On the other hand, the plantings that get the smiles, conversation, and attention of children may well be the most artistically effective.

TREE PLACEMENT

Let us look at some of the ways we can make better landscapes by studying the concept of depth.

The tree represented in **2–1** is alone. We recognize it as a tree by its general outline, a simple triangle. Its trunk is represented by a single vertical line. Even a child would recognize these primitive visual signals as a tree. What do we know about this "tree"? Actually, very little. We rely on other visual signals to tell us more. We do not know what kind of tree it is. We do not know how big it might be—or how faraway it is.

I am purposefully using such simple graphics to allow us to concentrate on the basic principles of depth and related visual signals. Any more complex representation of a tree would distract from key relationships and perhaps introduce complications that may be best sorted out once simple relationships of depth are understood. We perceive depth from a number of sources: texture, perspective, detail, and position. We can isolate

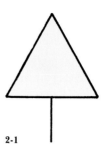

2-1

these visual signals and study them one at a time using these simple drawings.

The two trees represented in **2–2** are exactly the same size and shape. The eye picks up their images and has no reason to doubt that they are essentially the same. Let's pose a question, however. How do we know they are the same size? Is it possible that one of the trees is actually smaller, but closer to the viewer, thus exactly compensating for its smaller size? If so, which one?

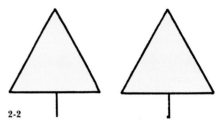

2-2

The visual signal is immediately complicated in **2–3** by overlapping one tree over the other. Now which tree is the larger one? The tree on the right must be bigger because it is farther away. Yet, it is the "same size" in the drawing. It is interesting to notice how our minds automatically sort out this information without any con-

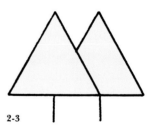

2-3

scious need to go through the logic of the biological phenomenon. We look at these two "trees" and the information is transferred from our eyes to some portion of our brain without our being aware of it happening at all. One of the key physiological and psychological principles at work here is called "prior experience." We have seen this view before. Our experience tells us that if we see two trees the same height, but one is farther away, the farther tree is actually taller. This is one fundamental concept of depth perception.

Which tree is the larger of the two represented in **2–4**? We are automatically tempted to choose the tree on the left; however, we have already been spoiled. We have already received previous information that the tree on the right might be farther away, and therefore, just as tall. Is the tree on the right farther away than the tree on the left? It's possible. What if I told you that the tree on the right was actually closer and quite a bit smaller than the tree on the left? After a moment's consideration, you would have to admit that there is insufficient evidence; you cannot tell. I agree, but you had to think about it for a bit, didn't you? It was not immediately obvious.

The tree on the right is a greater distance away in **2–5**. The drawing of it is, in actuality, smaller as well. The question arises, Is the tree on the right taller than the tree on the left? In the drawing, we can measure the trees and find the left tree taller, but our actual experience might suggest differently. When we view landscapes, the trees that are in the distance are always smaller. If we were to put a ruler down on a photograph of a landscape, we could measure off each tree, but only relative to the single scale of the ruler; we would not be able to measure which is the actual tallest tree, because we would not know which one to measure since the scale of measurement is different for each tree, depending on how near or far it is. I hope you see that we face a similar problem with this drawing. The distant tree "measures" smaller with a ruler, but is it *actually* smaller? It might be the same size or it might really be bigger; either way, the scale of measurement would have to be different for each tree since one is farther away from the viewer than the other.

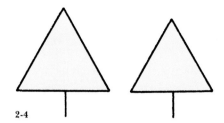

2-4

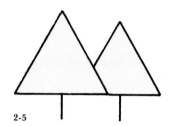

2-5

With these same two trees reversed in their front to back positions in **2–6**, the smaller tree on the right is quite obviously the smaller tree because we can both measure it with a ruler and observe that it logically must be smaller in the landscape as well, since it is closer to the viewer.

Let's introduce another visual depth signal in **2–7**. Which tree is the taller? Clearly, the tree on the right is the taller because, while it measures the "same size" as the tree on the left, it is farther away. What makes it appear farther away? The slight rise in the level of the lowest branches is the new visual signal. The trunks are the same length; therefore, the tree must be farther away. One could also argue that these trees might be the same size and are merely on a slope going down from right to left.

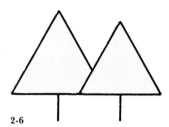

2-6

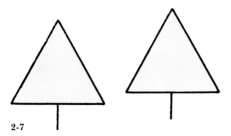

2-7

2-9

Two visual signals are simultaneously combined in **2–8**. Notice how one signal reinforces the other. The tree on the right is clearly in the background. The trunks are both the same length. The overlapping image, plus the increased height of the soil surface and bottom branches of the tree on the right, make it appear farther away. We still cannot determine the actual height of these trees. Are they the same size? Quite possibly. It is important to note here that the actual height of the tree really does not matter when it comes to the perception of depth. Perhaps an exaggerated example will serve to illustrate this better.

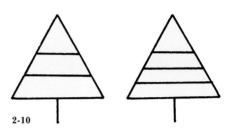

2-10

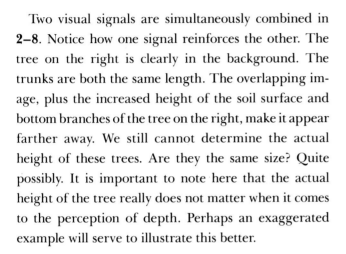

2-8

The two trees in **2–9** are obviously different when we measure them with the same simple ruler. The tree on the right measures smaller by about half. Yet, because of their positions, it is not clear which one is actually the smaller tree in the landscape. We have created an optical illusion or problem of sorts. With a few lines on a plain sheet of paper we are able to make a smaller tree look like a larger tree.

Other visual signals give clues as well. The two trees in **2–10** measure the same height, but have some new

features. The tree on the right has four increments of "height," whereas the tree on the left has only three. We do not exactly know what these increments represent, but the tree on the right looks "older." We are, perhaps, getting visual signals that suggest branches. I don't know. In any case, the tree on the right looks older and, therefore, taller. Since the shorter tree on the left "measures" the same height as the tree on the right, it must be closer. Our minds make these subtle adjustments—probably based on our prior experience—but without our really being aware of our thinking about it. If we were shopping for a Christmas tree, we would select the tree on the right because it has more branches—if the sections represent branches— and is, therefore, older and larger. We would not select the tree on the left because it probably contains gaps between its sparse branches, is too young and too small. What a difference one horizontal line makes!

ROCK PLACEMENT

I don't mean to belabor a point, but if the two squares in **2–11** represent rocks, how can you tell whether one is bigger than the other? They measure the same in the drawing, but how can you be sure that they are the same size? The rock on the right may be smaller and closer to the viewer. The rock on the left may be larger and farther away. The same signals that applied to trees also apply to rocks.

We can tell from the top drawing in **2–12** which rocks are bigger and which rocks are smaller. We also have a sense of which ones are close or farther away. But what about the lower pair of boxes with horizontal lines? It may surprise you that rocks have "increments" just as trees do. The nooks and crannies and surface texture of a stone gives us a lot of visual information that we are not always aware of. These two "rocks" have horizontal ledges, or striations, on them. Which rock is farther away? Most viewers would select the rock on the right. Which rock is bigger? Most would again select the rock on the right for the same reason: it has more striations, it is farther away; therefore, it is bigger.

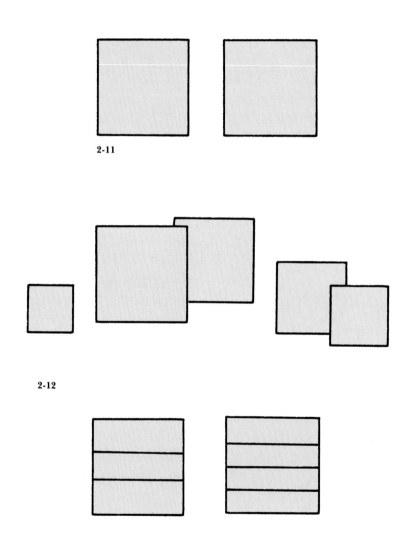

2-11

2-12

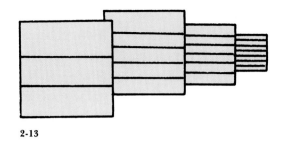

2-13

similar increments. In the foreground, we notice the cracks and shelves in the rocks' surfaces. As we look into the distance, these details get closer and closer together until they blend together into a plain grey or black color—just as in the drawing. Which is bigger, the "rock" on the far left or on the far right?

The series of "rocks" in **2–13** could just as well be wooden blocks, buildings, or windows. The principle remains the same. The incremental size displayed by these figures decreases with distance. When we view a tree up close, its branches are distinct and far apart. Trees farther and farther away have their branches closer and closer together. Even though the measured height of a tree in a photograph is less, the distant tree looks taller due to its smaller increments. Rocks have

DETAIL AND ITS CONTRIBUTION TO DEPTH

In the landscape painting shown in **2–14**, the artist has taken advantage of another visual phenomenon. As depth increases, the increment size decreases and decreases until objects appear fuzzy and unfocused. Indi-

2-14

vidual details become so compact that the eye blends them together into a medium grey. Notice the distinct trees in the foreground. Their branches are separate, and their trunks are obvious. On the other hand, when we see the same type and size of trees a half mile farther away in the middle distance, their trunks have become insignificant. The branch details are lost because the increments are so close together that the eye can no longer distinguish them. The painter could, presumably, with laser technology under high magnification, draw every single branch on these distant trees. But why? The "improved" painting would look the same because the eye still could not pick up the minute increments anyway. In the far distance there are trees also. We cannot see them, but we know they are there because the distant hills are not tall enough to be above the timberline. The trees are there. They are "hiding" in the mist, growing in the rock crevices, and following along the lower ridges where moisture collects.

The foreground trees seen in **2–15** are tall, distinct, and clearly described. A path with a human figure provides interest and scale. The middle distance contains bunched-up trees and rocks on the left. Just as in the previous example, we know trees are all along the edge of the bay; they are just too small in scale to be seen. Sometimes in the living bonsai landscape, we can represent these extremely small groves with just a touch of moss.

2-15

The same three views found in successful landscapes are easily identified along the river in **2–16**. Detail provides the foreground. Loss of detail, due to excessively small increments, forms the middle landscape; the hazy distant mountains finish the scene. A three-tree bonsai grove would represent only a portion of this foreground. A saikei of the same scene could contain the entire foreground as well as the middle and the distant landscapes.

The three trees in **2–17** are all Chinese elms. From left to right are *Seiju* elm, regular Chinese elm, and cork bark elm. Their differences can help us create depth. The three trees are planted in a straight line. No one of the trees is closer or farther from the viewer. We have already achieved some illusion of depth due to their relative sizes, internodes, leaf size, increment size, height of lowest branch, and color.

The trees are located in **2–18** into foreground, middle distance, and far distance in order to capture more depth. The position of the two forward trees in front of the soil mound further enhances this effect.

Additional depth has been created in **2–19** by adding stones to the foreground. The Number One tree is now clearly in front of the rocks. The Number Two tree—the middle landscape—is slightly hidden by the edge of one rock. The distant small tree is intentionally slightly out of focus by the camera lens to make it seem even farther away. The actual distance between tree Number One and tree Number Three is only five inches; yet, in the miniature landscape it appears to be more like fifty feet. Notice the standard inch-measuring tape shown in **2–20**.

The above principles can be applied to rocks as well. The three rocks in **2–21**—numbered two, one, and three from left to right—exhibit many of the same characteristics that we have previously used only on trees. Rock Number One, the tallest, has a layered facade with large hollows, niches, and horizontal grooves. The total number of increments—noticeable layers—number between six and ten, depending on how you count some of the smaller grooves. Its top is rugged, but not highly eroded. Rock Number Two has around fifteen smaller well-spaced increments, and its top is well

2-16

THE CONCEPT OF DEPTH

43

2-17

2-19

2-18

2-20

THE ART OF SAIKEI

rounded, giving the impression of erosion. Rock Number Three has so many horizontal increments that they are difficult to count. They number about fifty, but they are so small that they start to appear fuzzy or hazy. This is similar to what was happening to distant trees in the landscape paintings. Rock Number Three's top is mountain-shaped and well eroded. These three stones are standing side by side, but we can already perceive some degree of depth between them. Let's exaggerate this subtle effect by repositioning the stones in their appropriate positions.

With these rocks at their correct places relative to each other in **2–22**, a great deal of additional illusion of depth is achieved. The individual details of rock Number One are in the foreground. The mimicking horizontal layers of rock Number Two become a matching rocky ridge in the middle landscape. The fuzzy distant mountain is again slightly blurred by the lens of the camera, similar to what happens with the human eye.

Remember our three elm trees? We can strengthen the depth in this miniature landscape shown in **2–23** by having similar visual signals coming from both rocks and trees. If the trees were located in inappropriate locations, as in **2–24**, the effect would be confusing; the conflicting signals tend to cancel out the illusion of depth we were able to achieve.

2-21

2-23

2-22

2-24

THE CONCEPT OF DEPTH

DETERMINING THE BEST POSITION FOR SAIKEI MATERIAL

The rock shown in **2–25** is a highly detailed, nicely curved and textured rock that will make an excellent foreground stone. It is interesting and its angled strata make clear increments. It would be a poor choice for use as a medium-sized ridge or distant mountain.

The hollowed-out sandstone shown in **2–26** has an interesting color, texture, and slant. It is an excellent candidate for a foreground stone because of its clarity, interest, and highly visual increments. This would make a good stone at the base of a tropical fig or *Schefflera* with the tree planted in the ground to the left of the rock, and some of the aerial roots cascading down the rock from left to right.

The layered, red river rock shown in **2–27** is an excellent example of a medium-distance stone. If this rock were used in the foreground, the trees would have to be so small as to be insignificant. Notice how the rock naturally flows from left to right due to the subtle rise in the sedimentary layers in the rock itself. This rock also displays a natural green color due to lichens growing in cracks towards the top. This growth resembles a low-lying prostrate juniper growing on arid rim rock.

A highly striated sedimentary stone is shown in **2–28**. The great number of increments suggests that this would be best used as a medium-distance stone rather than a foreground stone. Imagine the height of the trees that would complement this cliff. Five windswept spruce would look very nice on top of this bold outcropping. The base of the rock is not hollowed out in a shape that resembles ocean erosion. This is more like what one would find in a windy gorge.

The quartz stone shown in **2–29** is definitely not a foreground or medium-distance stone. It is "Mt. Fuji." The crystal inclusions in the rock glisten like freshly fallen snow. By adding a few fir trees in the foreground, as shown in **2–30**, some additional soil, and a single fir tree to form the middle distance, you have a saikei made with only one rock.

2-25

2-26

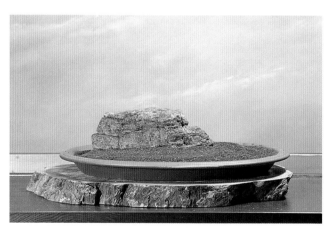

2-27

Close, medium, and far distances can be arranged in many ways, but the drawings in **2–31** show three of the most common. The numbered circles indicate the position in the oval tray, and the size of each circle corresponds to the height of each tree. The squares represent appropriate-sized and -detailed stones associated with the numbered trees. For larger group plantings, one might have five trees clustered together in position Number One, four trees at the Number Two position, and so forth. Assemble the groups with regard to their increment size, not their height. Group together similarly detailed trees and rocks for best results. Practice picking up random rocks and trees, and try to identify where they will look best.

Rocks that have an even, sponge-like texture, as found in some lava or pumice, are difficult to plant with proper consideration of their inherent depth. They offer the viewer few clues to their location. These rocks should be avoided. Instead, seek out richly textured and colored rock with contrast and oriented striations. These rocks contribute beautifully to the miniature landscape because they look like tiny natural outcrops or geologic formations.

Similarly with tree selection, seek out textured bark, roots that can be exposed, dead twigs, driftwood curves, snagged tops, and compact foliage. The medium-distance trees must be even smaller counterparts to the foreground "focus" trees. Do not be afraid to copy your front foliage with a completely different middle-distance species. The far distance can consist of only a single element—a solitary stone, the end of a winding path, a stream bank disappearing out of view, or even just hills of rolling moss. Attention to these three views of a landscape, grouping similar rocks and trees together, and close attention to the progressive compression of increments from the front of your container to the back will guarantee the visual success of your planting.

2-28

2-29

2-30

THE INFLUENCE OF COLOR

One further element that we need to consider is the role of color in the concept and perception of depth. Artists have for centuries noticed how objects in the distance appear to be more blue than the same objects nearby. We probably have all seen rolling hills in the distance. As each ridge disappears and then reappears again, we notice a definite color change. The lush greens of the foreground give way to increasing blue tones. The seated monk in **2–32** gazes out at the rich, warm brown colors of the opposite cliff and its waterfall. The distant hills are the same rock, but they appear blue because they are in the distance. The blue cast is thought to be related to the amount of particulate matter that we have to peer through in order to see into the distance. Light reflected from the distant hills tends to lose the red side of the spectrum as atmospheric impurities absorb or scatter those wavelengths. Notice the similar effect

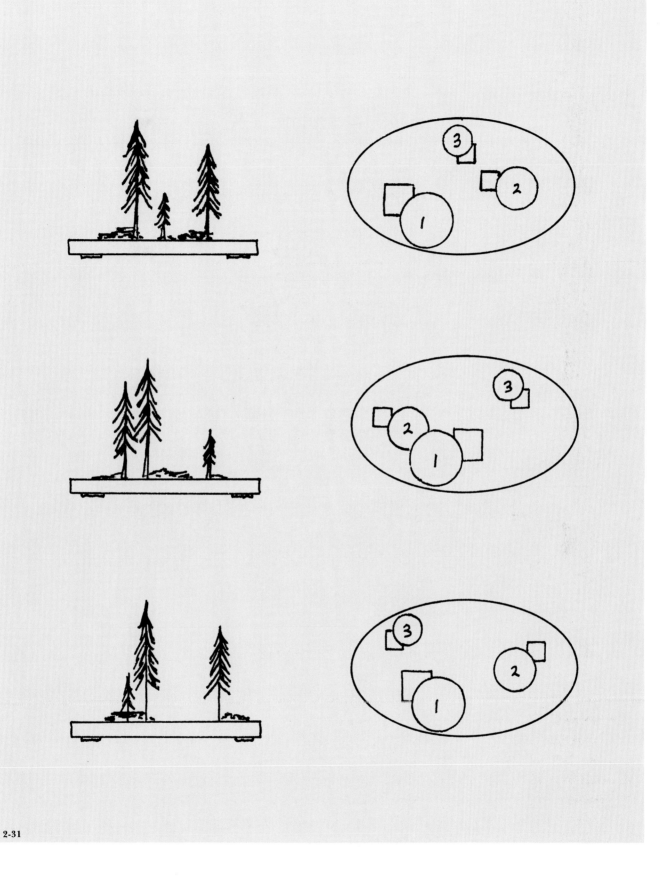

THE CONCEPT OF DEPTH

2-32

THE ART OF SAIKEI

50

2-33

2-34

when the monk looks down at the streamside deciduous grove encased in its own mist.

The distant mountains in **2–33** are bluer when compared to the foreground. In your miniature landscapes, you can take advantage of this same visual phenomenon.

The three rocks shown in **2–34** demonstrate the effect of color on the eye. The rocks are positioned side by side, yet the reddish rock in the middle appears closer.

The slightly darkish blue rock on the right seems farthest away, and the medium beige rock on the left appears to be situated somewhere in between. The saikei designer can take advantage of this optical illusion in conjunction with any of the other principles of depth perception that we covered earlier in this chapter. The best landscapes are able to incorporate all of these visual signals to create the most convincing illusion of depth.

3

THE FIVE ELEMENTS OF LANDSCAPE STYLE

The creative process is delicate, tenuous, and extremely difficult to understand, much less to teach to others. It has been said that the artist who learns basic technique first develops personal style first. Some budding artists reject this preliminary step because they fear it inhibits personal style rather than enhances it. I firmly believe that a solid background in history, technique, materials, and methods provides the path of least resistance to the creative process. Therefore, I want to explore what I consider to be the fundamental concepts important to the creation of a good landscape—the five elements of landscape style: harmony, consistency, balance, scale, interest.

HARMONY

Harmony is defined as "the just adaptation of parts in any system to each other or the combination of things intended to form a connected whole." It is difficult to discuss harmony without looking at its opposite or its absence. If one aspect of a work of art "sticks out like a sore thumb," the art is not likely to be in harmony.

When we travel through natural landscapes, we might get a sense of the harmony of nature. Perhaps, we might also observe how certain aspects of human intervention do not harmonize. This might be the roadside stump of a tree, a power line, or a shopping mall. We may recognize these things as different, out of context, or disagreeable somehow. In more natural areas, temporarily out of the reach of these incongruous interventions, the landscape can evoke a deep sense of harmony. The rugged cliffs support windswept trees. Peaceful glens grow lush ferns. Snowy peaks produce the alpine fir, and the tall blades of beach grass wave incessantly on the dunes.

It is difficult to grasp through logic why a tree harmonizes with the rock next to it. To some degree, the same forces shape both. It is possible to go into the mountains and see a rock leaning to the right next to a tree leaning to the left. But would we take a photograph of that tree and rock? Would we paint them? Would we try to duplicate them in our landscape? I don't think it's very likely.

Our eyes would pass over the scene probably without even being conscious of it. It is more likely that we might, instead, notice a tree growing next to a rock that leaned in the same direction. I tend to focus on what I find pleasing myself. I will come across a beautiful natural arrangement in the wilderness—a rock terrace with draping ground cover, wild flowers, and compact shrubbery topped off with a magnificently shaped pine tree. I'll gaze at this little natural scene and wish to reproduce it in my own backyard. But why this particular spot? Why not a place 100 yards to the left? The natural landscape 100 yards away is very much a part of the scheme of nature. It is simply that not all of what is "natural" is equally beautiful to our eyes. Some parts are more pleasing than others. They hold our attention longer. They seem to harmonize.

The rock shown in **3–1** has a natural depression that would contain a tree quite nicely. Its base is flared out slightly, its curves are gentle, and it is a rich color— combining brown and grey earth tones. The slender pine tree, *Pinus mugho rostrata*, shown in **3–2** has gentle curves like the rock. It has an interesting root that flares out at its base, and its bark color matches some of the grey color found in the stone's surface. Let's put these together as a simple rock planting.

The rock serves as the container as well as the harmony for the curves of the young pine tree (see **3–3**). The total planting has a greater impact than the rock alone or the tree alone. One element forms a relationship with the other so that they become inseparable. The tree, however, needed some trimming and wiring in order to closely match the contours of the rock.

Above, we took a rock and matched it to a tree. We can also take a tree and find an appropriate rock to go with it. If the spruce tree in **3–4** were growing on top of a rock, how would the rock be shaped? I think it should rise slightly on the right just like this tree's apex. It should exhibit left-to-right movement, although not strong enough to consider it windswept. Spruce trees do not like their roots in water, so the rock could not look like sandstone or beach rock. Let's try the lava rock shown in **3–5**.

The combined planting shown in **3–6** harmonizes

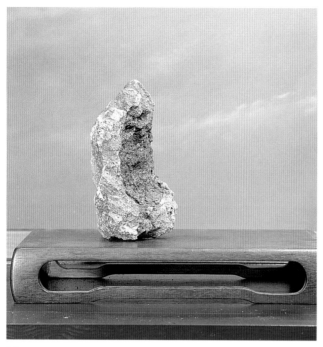

3-1

3-2

3-3

THE ART OF SAIKEI

54

3-4

3-5

well. The curves of the rock are mimicked by the tree. The brown color of the trunk is found in the earth tones of the rock. They both have a slight amount of left-to-right movement. The rock and the tree each do not look as well alone as they do together; the whole is greater than the sum of its parts.

Another element within the concept of harmony, the color of the container and its relationship to the saikei planting, must be addressed. From bonsai we have learned that most conifers look best in an earth brown pot. When a pine tree is planted in a blue-glazed container, the eyes are drawn towards the pot instead of the tree. Similarly with landscapes, unless the scene contains bright color from fruits, flowers, berries, or leaves,

the traditional earth brown pot seems best suited. Color in a planting can come from many sources, such as gravel, stones, trees, or soil. Small shrubs, mosses, or grasses can add various tones of green-blue or floral decoration. Try to select a container that complements all these hues.

CONSISTENCY

In some respects, the concept of consistency promotes harmony. Where there is consistency, there is often harmony as well. There are some subtle differences. *Consistency* is defined as "a standing together; a being fixed in union. Agreement of all of the parts of a complex thing with itself; congruity." These so-called agreements would certainly include having the same type of rocks in a planting; basalt and sandstone don't go together—unless you find a piece of sandstone actually intruded with a layer of basalt, the only way they would be found together in the natural landscape. If some stones are striated, then they all should be. Their colors should be very similar, only their sizes should differ.

We would not find cactus and ferns growing together in the woods. Neither would we plant orchids growing on oak trees. Yet we see countless examples of windswept bonsai with the soil in their containers covered with moss. This is inconsistent. Every natural landscape has a degree of logic. The elements that form this logic must be consistent with each other. I recommend that you always try to form a story about your planting. How did it form? How long ago? How old are the trees? What action formed the rocks? Would you find all these plants together naturally? If you can answer these questions, then your landscape has passed the basic "litmus test" for consistency.

We have learned from bonsai that if one tree is slanted, all the tress must slant. If the Number One branch grows upwards at twenty degrees above the horizontal, so must all the other branches. We often neglect extending these innate consistencies to rocks. If our Number One rock has a horizontal apex, then all the

3-6

other rocks must. If one stone leans left to right, then all the others must lean left to right. Notice the similarities in color, texture, lean, grain, and apex in all the rocks in **3–7**—from the foreground through the middle distance, all the way to the distant mountain range.

Even though we are producing a three-dimensional planting, we have to choose the viewing point from which the landscape is to be enjoyed. The fronts of all the trees are aligned towards this point. If ten trees all have their fronts forward and one tree faces backwards,

it becomes highly noticeable. All trees in a landscape are subject to the same wind, sun, rain, and other natural conditions. If one tree does not conform, it looks out of place; it is inconsistent. When exposed rootage is a design factor, all trees should have some degree of exposed rootage. Similarly, if only one tree in a grouping has a dead top, it looks like some random act of violence. It is better to restate your idea a few more times to reinforce it. The presence of *jin* and *shari* on only one tree seems out of place. Why just this one tree? Why not

秀水

明川惠九〇年

3-7

THE FIVE ELEMENTS OF LANDSCAPE STYLE

3-8

THE ART OF SAIKEI

some of the others? In bonsai, we are left feeling uneasy when we view a tree with only one dead branch. It implies that the owner not only failed to care for the bonsai properly, but also did not even cut off the dead branch before the show. A similar tree, with a dead top, two dead branches and some peeled, driftwood accents on the trunk, provides the viewer with a logical explanation for this tree's condition: it is living in a tough environment.

Miniature landscapes can make visual sense in a similar way through duplication, repetition, and reiteration. We reinforce our ideas by stating them again and again in different ways. For example, a harsh climate might be expected to contain distorted trees, angular rock, unpolished gravel, lichens rather than moss, lots of *jin*, *shari*, and *sabamiki*, dead twigs littering the ground, and low ground cover. By contrast we would expect a wet, still, and protected landscape to have straight trees, rounded rocks, polished gravel, moss, ferns, lush green foliage, flowers, and elaborate shrubs. Consistent elements reinforce each other. A single inconsistency might not be immediately obvious, but the viewer may get a certain uneasy feeling about the planting. It just does not look right, but you can't put your finger on why.

Complex plantings with a foreground, middle distance, and background have an additional problem: their respective landscapes within the greater landscape must pass the consistency test as well. In the landscape shown in **3—8** the shape of the trees in the foreground reflects their calm location. In the middle-distance landscape the trees' shape correctly represents the higher altitude, the rocky soil, and the increased wind. In this case it would not be proper to simply transplant the foreground trees to the middle ground or to the background.

For an effective foreground, study the conditions that are present, then assemble the appropriate combination of rocks, soil, moss, gravel, trees, and understory. If your middle distance represents a subtle change in climate, then adjustments will have to be made. The middle-distance landscape is not always just a "miniature" version of the foreground. Similarly, the background may be a different climate again. A snowcapped peak has no vegetation. A distant cliff may be windswept while the middle ground represents a streamside environment. Treat these views separately for the best results.

BALANCE

Balance is the mental act of comparing or estimating two or more elements against each other. The bonsai shown in **3—9** is planted on the left side of the container. You can easily see why it was not planted on the right side of the pot. Most viewers would also agree that if this tree were planted in the exact middle of the bonsai pot, it would still not be balanced. If we were to place this pot on top of a balance beam we could determine where the exact center of gravity is located. The exact center of

3-9

3-10

mass of this planting is marked by the white chalk in **3–10**. I asked a group of fifteen people to estimate where they thought the center of balance was in this planting. All selections came within an inch of the purple chalkline. Why the difference? I think that when we "weigh" visual mass, we tend to take factors into account that have no actual mass at all. The strongest of these visual factors is visual movement. When we see a tree or a rock with strong visual movement from left to right, we tend to "weigh" the visual space to the right of the object. This space obviously has no weight itself, but we are content to place the object farther to the left. For example, in **3–11** the rock seems comfortable in this container when positioned one-third of the way from left to right. When the same rock is rotated around to expose its hollowed-out cave, the same position in the container feels unbalanced. This rock in **3–12** is positioned, rather, one-quarter of the way from left to right. Thus, we have taken into account the additional "weight" of the space to the right of the rock.

Without actually being aware of it, we are constantly weighing and averaging individual components in paintings, sculpture, and landscapes. If we think we have too many tall pieces of furniture on one side of the living room, it bothers us. If color is not evenly distributed in a painting, it may be uncomfortable. We attempt to fill bare areas of walls with wall hangings. We may try to contrast light upholstery with darker pillows. In our lives, many of us are constantly adjusting our visual world to get things back into balance. Just as it would be simplistic to actually weigh the furniture in your living room, it is inappropriate to put your bonsai pot on a balance beam. If it balances visually, that is the balance we are interested in; it is balanced. Period.

In your landscapes strive to obtain a mix of the height, weight, size, and position of your stones. Your trees should exemplify the broad range of size found in nature from old to young. Evenly spaced trees look like an orchard or plantation. Allow their positions to be more random for a natural effect. When your planting is finished, as a rule of thumb the overall visual balance should center itself one-third of the way in from one side of the container. Balance colors, textures, materials, and

3-11

3-12

positions. Weigh the empty areas against the filled areas, the light against the dark. The finished miniature landscape will have a pleasant sense of asymmetry, of random position, yet at the same time appear balanced, controlled, and predictable.

SCALE

No representation of a landscape can be successful without careful attention to scale. The comparative sizes of trees to rocks, trees to moss, rocks to gravel, etc., are fundamental in creating the miniature landscape. We are seeking to create an optical illusion. Without careful attention to the relative sizes of elements in the landscape, we destroy this illusion. We must consider the canopy versus its understory. Are the rhododendrons the proper size to be located under those fir trees? Are those ferns too big? If a tree is seen at a distance, it is imperative that its proper size be carefully considered. Study natural landscapes. Take a measuring tape to a photograph of a landscape. Sometimes the actual size of a tree is deceiving to the eye. A distant oak tree might have to be only one inch tall to be in scale with its surroundings.

Watch the scale of your container as well. Previously, I described the value of a simple drawing in planning your landscape. Imagine, if you can, containers of different sizes and shapes around your miniature landscape. Is the container the right height? Should it be oval or rectangular? Is its color and texture appropriate? The size, shape, color, and texture of a container can add to or detract from the scale of the entire planting.

Consider all aspects of the planting when considering scale. Flower size sometimes will eliminate a shrub or tree. Choose the size of your gravel to fit the needs of the planting; the gravel should not look like small boulders, nor should it look like insignificant sand. The surface detail in your stones should match the trees' surface detail; a great amount of detail should be seen in both, or not in both. If you can see many cracks and crevices in the rocks, but you cannot see twigginess in the branches of adjacent trees, the scale may be off.

The use of unusual rocks is admirable in saikei; however, some types of stones should be avoided. Fossils can add a fascination to stones and we can get great pleasure out of seeing the ancient remains of creatures in them; nevertheless, we may find the use of such stones—to create sea cliffs, for example—to be limited. Imagine enjoying a miniature seacoast saikei only to discover a fossil the relative size of a mastodon washed up on the "beach." Some fossil inclusions are just too far out of scale to work in miniature landscapes. For the same reason, I recommend avoiding such objects as seashells, petrified wood, arrowheads, and the like. Most clay and mud figurines are out of scale as well. When in doubt, measure them. Are they an appropriate size? If not, eliminate them or choose something else.

INTEREST

Of all the five elements of landscape style, *interest* is the hardest to explain. The word is defined as "to gain the attention of or to excite; to engage or to induce us to take part in; curiosity." I once labored to satisfy a student who was particularly exasperating. He had decided that his profession was precise and detailed and that bonsai would be a good hobby for him because he possessed just those exacting qualities necessary for success. We created, destroyed, created, and adjusted a maple grove so many times I thought I was going to go crazy! No three trees could be in a single line. No two trees could be the same height. The distances between the trees had to be all different. The trunks all had to curve in the same manner. There must not be any crossing branches or eye-poking branches. The planting had to be balanced from the front, both sides, and the back. This went on for about five hours. In the end, the planting satisfied all criteria but one: interest. The planting was as boring as its creator.

In the natural bridge landscape that we will develop in Chapter Six (refer to page **118**), the obvious interest is the bridge itself. In an otherwise dull desert planting, an incredible natural phenomenon is created. This is interesting. In various natural landscapes that we enjoy, there is always some element that is unpredictable. I enjoy a particular ocean location at sundown because the sun's rays poke through a hole in an offshore rock. This isn't to say that a seacoast scene needs this element. This unusual aspect at this particular beach makes the landscape more interesting. The sun's rays shining through that gap grabs my attention, and makes the landscape special.

In many forms of art, the appearance of the incongruous makes the signature of the artist. The "flaw," or the "imperfection," can be associated directly with the artist. In oriental carpets, the artist intentionally includes a flaw in the design. This might be a dropped stitch or an imperfection in a border. I find it fascinating that the inclusion of a defect somehow keeps the carpet maker humble. Carpet purveyors seek out this flaw as they might look for a signature on a painting. This tradition is found in the Chinese Literati School of landscape art. The flaw becomes the interest or the signature. The artist has intentionally caught the eye of the beholder—has excited curiosity.

As we work in the particular art form of saikei, let us not lose sight of this most important concept: if you have something to say, then say it. What aspect of this planting held your interest? Have you communicated this interest to the viewer? If not, why not? Sometimes the best part about a landscape is its incongruous quality. Exaggerate your statement in order to communicate it to others. This esoteric side of landscaping is what makes it special. It is the fantasy and the signature at the same time. It is your *bunjin*. Take advantage of it; it is your art.

4

TOOLS AND EQUIPMENT

PRUNING TOOLS

A sampling of the many pruning tools that are available through bonsai supply nurseries are shown in **4–1**. These eight tools all have specific functions, and I will describe these beginning from top to bottom.

First, the top large tool is designed to cut through heavy wood. Its English common names vary widely from **root pruner** to **branch splitter**. The cutting jaws are wide and will not pinch together during compression like the more common **concave cutter** (the second tool). Notice how the cutting surfaces join together. There is no metal to get in the way when a large or difficult cut is made. They function equally well as root cutters. The edges are not as sharp as most pruning tools; therefore, they are safe to use in sandy soils.

The second tool is the so-called **concave cutter**. Actually, two tools cut in the desirable concave fashion: this one and the tool that follows. Most cuts on trees will not heal well because of swelling of the cambium layer. These tools do a superior job of removing excess wood so that the wound heals rapidly, with a minimum of permanent scarring.

Tool number three is a **spherical knob cutter**. Its jaw design enables the user to cut as deeply past the cambium layer as possible. The wound heals quickly, minimizing scarring, and thereby helping the tree protect itself from insects and disease.

The fourth tool down is a **miniature concave cutter**, especially suitable for miniature bonsai or miniature landscapes. The tiny cutting edges allow it to fit into small spaces, yet the power from the large handles is great. I recommend this tool for saikei and especially for those with arthritic or small hands.

Tool number five is commonly used as a **leaf trimmer** in bonsai work, but thanks to its rapid speed, versatility, and low cost, it makes a wonderful starting tool for those wanting to work with the small plant material associated with miniature landscapes.

The sixth tool down in **4–1** is perhaps the most common bonsai tool known. The simple design of the **shears** makes it possible to trim plants at any speed. They are easily sharpened, cleaned, and maintained. The tips of

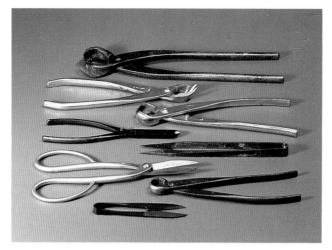

4-1

the shears will cut the smallest of twigs; yet fairly large branches can be cut close to the handles.

The seventh tool is a **miniature spherical knob cutter**. It is especially useful when working on saikei or miniature landscape material. Its cutting action is similar to tool number three except that the smaller size of this tool enables it to get into cramped spaces.

The last tool, the bottom one in **4–1,** is a **finger-held leaf trimmer**, which is very useful for rapid and repeated small cuts on miniature plant material. Normally used to defoliate maple trees on bonsai, this small tool is useful for trimming miniature landscape trees and small bonsai. It is self-sharpening, requires little or no maintenance, and is the least expensive of these tools.

TWEEZERS

The human hand is large and clumsy when working with miniature bonsai and miniature landscapes. Six grasping tools are shown in **4–2** that can be of help. I will describe them from top to bottom.

Perhaps the least expensive and most useful bonsai tool in the world is the **chopstick**. I have had many years' practice in the use of these two wooden devices, dating back to when I was a ten-year-old trying to use them in a Chinese restaurant. Eventually, you become

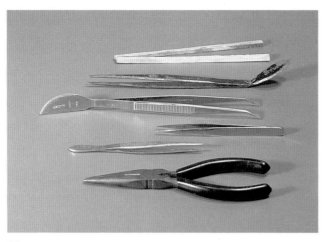

4-2

skilled enough so that you can pick up a single grain of rice without effort. Chopsticks are used in bonsai to compress soil during potting and repotting, to pick insects off the branches, to pluck debris from the soil surface, to test for dryness in the container, and to rub bark off of *jin*. Small stakes made of chopstick wood can act as supports for twine or as fine copper wire supports. A small piece of wood can be inserted into a loop of wire to create a turnbuckle. Save used chopsticks from your Chinese meal or invest a few cents and get a brand-new pair!

The **tweezers** below the chopsticks are thirty years old; they still function as well as a new pair. They are **Japanese bonsai tweezers with a spatula** on the opposite end. They are useful for picking up debris, helping to thread some twine around a branch, untie a knot, squash aphids, and pluck old pine needles off that have turned brown. The spatula end compresses and shapes soil in landscapes like a miniature hoe. Its sharp edge assists in separating lateral roots from the edge of the container prior to repotting.

Tool number three is a **tweezer variation** on the one above it, except that it is made with stainless steel. This metal, of course, does not rust. The edges of the spatula stay sharper longer, and one edge of the spatula is intentionally blunt and *never* should be sharpened. This area on the tool is designed for rubbing or scraping when cutting is undesirable. This side of the spatula is used whenever damage should be kept to a minimum.

The next two **smaller tweezers** differ only slightly from each other. The bottom one has its jaws slightly serrated and roughened up on the inside for greater traction and hold. Otherwise, they are identical. Use either of these two tools for any delicate job where hands alone are too big or clumsy—such as applying a drop of glue, removing a scale insect, threading wire through a lead sinker, removing blossom debris, or rubbing out unwanted buds.

The last tool, at the bottom of **4–2**, is simply a pair of **needlenose pliers**. They are included with this group because sometimes we run across a job that is too tough for the tweezers. These pliers have a small pair of jaws that are not much bigger than the tweezers; yet you can apply a great deal more force because of the increased leverage provided by the pliers' handles. Use to crimp wire for added strength, smash slug eggs, grip a strip of bark for tearing, poke a hole in the soil for a copper guy wire. Anywhere the tweezer is a little too weak, use the needlenose pliers.

BRUSHES

The top brush shown in **4–3** is a common **painter's trim brush**. It is inexpensive and designed for latex paint. It measures one inch across the face of the natural bristles. This brush is useful for sweeping large areas of soil on a miniature landscape. It can be used to apply mineral oil to landscape rocks for added sheen. It cleans up small messes on the work surface.

The next two brushes in **4–3** are **disposable foam-type brushes** found in most paint stores. They can function, when dry, as small "bulldozers" to even out soil levels. Their resilient working tips do not deflect as easily as fibre or bristle brushes. Perhaps their best use is in the application of oil-based stains, bleaches, or lime sulfur to work surfaces. *Beware:* most Danish oil finishes will spontaneously combust when heavy deposits and residues are left in the brush or rag. These brushes do not have to be cleaned as such; just soak them for a day in plain water to eliminate the chance of fire, then throw them away while they are still wet. I dislike cleaning brushes, so whenever I apply smelly or noxious

4-3

the large size of the previous brushes makes them inappropriate for fine and detailed work. These brushes will go into crevices where others will not. You can use them to apply pesticides to the tops of scale insects, clean out small cracks in bark or rocks, paint on lime sulfur along a curving *jin*, and even insert insecticide into a burrowing insect's hole. The brushes are readily available, relatively inexpensive, and come in an infinite variety of sizes and shapes.

SCOOPS

The creation of miniature bonsai landscapes requires the addition of soils and gravels in copious quantities as compared to bonsai. A four-foot tray that is two inches deep requires a lot of material. Soil scoops make this transfer easier. The mess that results from trying to pour soil from a small plastic bucket into a saikei pot is enormous. Soil scoops are available in all sizes to help in this effort.

The top two **cast-aluminum scoops** shown in **4–4** are available from feed and seed stores. They are used primarily to dispense grass seed, bulk kitty food, and obscure stuff like sorghum and rolled millet. They are available in sizes ranging from around a cupful to nearly

bleaches, oils, or paints, I like the convenience of the inexpensive disposable brush.

The next two brushes down in **4–3** are **stencil brushes**. Their short, compact yet soft bristles are ideal for shaping and packing soil particles around rocks. They help greatly in forming land contours. When dry, their cleansing action on bark removes dust, scaly debris, and loose dirt. When wet, they can be used to scrub rocks and roots to cleanse them of mud and slime. They are useful when large areas of driftwood pieces need to be treated with lime sulfur.

The **small white cosmetics brush** towards the bottom left of **4–3** is normally used to apply blush or powder to the face. This small brush is extremely fine-bristled and can be a useful tool to clean dust and debris from delicate work. In situations where most brushes are found to be too coarse, too aggressive, and too clumsy, this small brush is perfect.

The brown fibre brush on the middle to lower right is the traditional **Japanese bonsai brush**. It has bristles which are coarse and inflexible like what you might find on a whisk broom. It moves much soil and cleans up a lot of messes. It functions best to smooth the soil surface after repotting and to clean soil particles from the surface of rocks and the edges of the container. As your work gets smaller and more detailed, you may find this brush a little crude.

The four blue-handled brushes at the bottom of **4–3** are **artist's brushes** designed for watercolor use. Often,

4-4

half a gallon per scoopful. They are lightweight aluminum, never rust, and will last a lifetime; a worthy investment.

The three nearly **cylindrical scoops** in the middle are of Japanese manufacture. They are stainless steel sheet metal and have a flat, closed end that allows them to stand up like the example on the left. The thin stainless sheet metal easily penetrates soil better than the cast-aluminum scoops above. When applying gravel or soil a little at a time, the stand-up feature of the Japanese scoops is a definite plus. A half-full aluminum scoop, when set down on the table, tends to become an empty scoop all by itself.

The **plastic homemade scoop** on the bottom left of **4–4** is made by gluing two pieces of PVC pipe together. The two pieces were cut on a mitre box and joined with super glue. This simple scoop delivers soil or gravel to the miniature landscape as efficiently as the others. It is a bit harder to load, however.

The two **silver spoons** on the lower right function well as scoops for delivering small amounts of gravel to a stream bed. The use of chicken grit, crushed quartz, or limestone must be limited and carefully placed for best results. These spoons work well to separate gravel colors from each other, acting as a plow and general picker-upper. They can be used also to stir linseed oil, Danish oil finish, latex paint, or to make muck (refer to Chapter Seven)—but they must be carefully washed and returned to the silverware drawer before they are discovered missing—to avoid spousal conflict!

WIRE

Traditional Chinese training of *P'en T'sai* did not involve the use of wire. New buds were allowed to grow in the desired direction of growth. Where growth was not wanted, the emerging buds were removed while they were still young and succulent. Japanese horticulture, since the nineteenth century, has promoted the use of wire to train branches on bonsai material. On smaller plant material, such as what is used in miniature bonsai or saikei, wire becomes less necessary. For larger bonsai,

4-5

it is a technique readily accepted by the masters. The choice remains up to you.

A variety of sizes of copper wire are shown in **4–5**. The best wire to use is **solid annealed copper**—sometimes called soft copper wire. As the wire is wound around the branch to be trained, the wire looses its softness. The branch is moved into place and after a few months the wire can be removed by cutting it off. Normally this is done in early summer. If a branch requires further training, it can be wired into place again in early fall. The most useful gauges of copper wire range from 28 gauge to 4 gauge; the lower the gauge, the thicker the wire. The most appropriate sizes for miniature bonsai or saikei are gauges 28, 26, 24, 22, and 20.

Copper-clad aluminum wire from Japan is available in most bonsai nurseries. This wire will work, but is generally considered inferior because of its poor strength. It takes more aluminum wire to bend a branch than copper wire.

WATERING DEVICES

There are many ways to water your bonsai, miniature bonsai, or miniature landscape. The best method is the method that is easiest for you. For best results, water

4-6

ters. You control the pressure with your hand on every squeeze, so you can be cautious on your rock planting and yet be aggressive on your bonsai. This sprayer is a must for potting and repotting. I always have one handy during workshops to help keep roots moist during transplanting. To fertilize your plantings, add liquid fertilizer to the water solution at the rate of one teaspoon per gallon. Never add granules to this bottle since they will clog the spraying device.

The **long hose-end sprayer** in the foreground of **4–6** is a popular device for watering sensitive plants, flowers, and container gardens. It connects to your hose, and offers a fine mist coming from the rose at the end of the sprayer. The trigger serves as an off–on switch and controls the water force as well. If you wish to keep the sprayer in a continuous spraying mode, a latch will lock the trigger open. You cannot fertilize with this sprayer.

For just a few dollars, the **blue rose** in the middle foreground of **4–6** is the simplest, most trouble-free device ever invented. It attaches to the end of your hose and you control the force of the spray with the hose faucet handle itself. You can drop it, kick it, freeze it, and even fail to clean it, and it will continue to work. If you wish to fertilize, simply add your liquid fertilizer drops to an indoor watering can, dilute, and water once a week with that.

lightly early in the day, and then repeat about ten minutes later. Do not water a bonsai once and walk away. The water will not penetrate to where the moisture will benefit the roots. In the rear of **4–6** is a commercially available **hose-end sprayer** that can be useful for watering many bonsai. Stand at least fifteen feet away and let the scattered spray hit the leaves, branches, pots, and bonsai bench. Wait about ten minutes and do it again. The container is designed to dispense fertilizer, and it does this as well. Once a week, a teaspoon of liquid or granular fertilizer, placed in the hose-end container, will help the plants grow quite nicely. Always use a fertilizer that is lower in nitrogen as compared to phosphorus or potassium, such as 5-10-10.

The large container on the left of **4–6** is a **compact compressed-air sprayer**. For small plants or for few plants, this is all you need. It will hold a gallon of water, and, after being pumped up with the built-in inflator, it will deliver moisture to your miniature bonsai at a predictable and controllable rate of pressure. This device is particularly well suited for rock plantings and extremely small bonsai. To apply fertilizer, just add a few drops of 10-10-10 liquid to the water, and spray.

The **hand-operated spray bottle** on the right in **4–6** is the least expensive watering equipment you can buy. These spray bottles can be found in most garden cen-

THE GROWING BENCH

Locate a suitable place in your yard where at least four hours of sunlight penetrates each day. The **bench** will offer protection from sun scalding if it is located in a shady area between the hours of 2 P.M. and 4 P.M. in the summer. A good bench will be about 40 inches off the ground. It is, of course, level and will provide a good-looking, welcome sight to the garden. Provide shade for the hottest months and winter protection with plastic sheeting and heat, if necessary. Treat your shelf each year with half-strength household bleach, which destroys most overwintering insects and disease. Pots may be wired to the bench to discourage theft, if necessary.

THE WORK TABLE

The best **work table** I have used is an old solid-core door laid down on an old desk. The door provided enough elbow room to work comfortably and the desk provided the drawers necessary for tool storage, aprons, spray bottles, wire, and rags. Soil and gravel can be stored underneath in plastic tubs, pails, or small garbage cans. Supply each container with its own scoop for convenience. A heavy **turntable** in the middle of your workbench is a necessity. The turntable shown in **4–7** is one of my favorites. Handmade from plywood twenty years ago, it is not as handsome as it used to be, but it still functions well. The two front drawers open for tools that are commonly used, and a stop on the side keeps the rotating surface still when you do not want it to move.

The **two turntables** shown in **4–8** are available through bonsai supply nurseries. The black one is Japanese and has a heavy cast-iron base. The knob on the front controls rotation of the turntable. Its stout plywood rotating surface is heavily laminated and will resist moisture because of the marine-type glue used in its construction. The wooden brown turntable is of United States manufacture, made of western red cedar. The table surface is controlled by friction rather than by the use of a screw or wing-nut apparatus (see **4–9**).

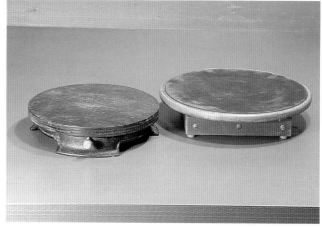

4-8

4-9

4-7

GROWING CONTAINERS

You can build your own temporary growing containers from wood. The bottom tray shown in **4–10** is a **homemade box** nailed together using old cedar fencing material. It provides excellent drainage and conforms to the generally flat shape conducive to the propagation of cuttings, seedlings, and young raft-styled maples and junipers. It is large enough to hold a complete miniature landscape for a year, while revisions and substitutions are being considered. The container just above it, the beige one, is a **plastic container** actually designed for cheese production. Its proportions and size make it an ideal training pot for collected trees and rock plantings. You have to drill several holes in the bottom for drainage. The brick-red **plastic pot** is commonly found in florists' shops and nurseries that sell "color spots" for the garden. It is made to imitate the more expensive red clay pots. Its wide surface area and cupped shape make it ideal as a transitional bonsai pot for plant specimens that need another year of training before they can be promoted to a bonsai pot or saikei tray. The top pot shown in **4–10** is a three-gallon dark green **plastic nursery container**. Most nursery containers are taller than they are wide. This particular size seems to be the exception. You can develop a strong rootage as well as an established trunk line in pots such as these, while getting trees ready for more expensive containers.

If you must grow your prospective material in the ground, I recommend placing a rock or concrete stepping stone on the ground first. Then place the developing bonsai or saikei plant on top of the rock. Mound a pile of well-draining leaf mould or garden mulch around the roots of your plant until the stone is completely covered. The new roots will love it! The heat from the rotting leaves will warm the roots, and the rock

will prevent them from going deep at the same time. Check on your planting from time to time. It may need additional moisture compared to the surrounding plants, but it will require less moisture than your plants that are in pots.

HOW TO MAKE A SIMPLE WOODEN LANDSCAPE TRAY

As you shop for Japanese containers in which to arrange your saikei, you will no doubt be dismayed at the cost of a large flat tray. In the interest of making it possible for you to pursue this fascinating hobby without going to exorbitant expense, I will show how to make a simple wooden tray for less than about fifteen dollars. A similar-sized imported saikei tray would run more than thirty times that cost!

Begin by cutting out a pleasing rectangular shape from one-half-inch marine-grade plywood (see **4–11**).

4-11

4-10

Do not use interior plywood; the glue is not waterproof and the plywood will delaminate itself in just a few months' watering. Make sure you allow enough room to obtain an illusion of depth. For a two-foot-long tray, allow at least sixteen inches of depth from front to back.

The sides are made of one-inch by two-inch moulding

strips (see **4–12**). Rough-sawn cedar is best because it lasts well exposed to weather and it absorbs wood stains better than hemlock, fir, or pine. Cut the strips to length (see **4–13**). Start with the short sides of the rectangle, and cut the two short pieces flush with the front and back edges of the bottom piece. The viewer will then be provided with an uninterrupted strip of wood along the front of the finished tray.

The finished top should look like **4–14** after some small strips are added just inside the lower corners to provide short legs.

The underside of the tray is shown in **4–15**. Note the additional long strip of moulding along the midline of the container. This strip provides additional support; remember that the accumulation of rocks, gravel, soil, and water can add up quickly. It is not uncommon to finish a planting this size and have to ask for assistance in order to move it!

An additional strip along the top edge, as shown in **4–16**, provides interest and gives a little more depth in the tray for larger trees and rocks, but it is entirely optional. If you have to bury your rocks a bit, you will find the extra height of this strip quite necessary.

A dark walnut Danish oil finish has been applied to an already completed tray shown in **4–17**. Notice how the color faintly resembles the earth brown tones found on Japanese bonsai containers. This color goes especially well with broadleaf evergreens and conifers.

To allow drainage for your container, simply drill holes in the plywood (see **4–18**). I find that a drill bit size of one-quarter inch works well. The holes are not so small that they get plugged up with soil, nor are they so big that the soil just pours through. These drain holes do not seem to weaken the plywood; so I recommend about ten holes per square foot. I find that the plywood lasts longer if the holes are treated with a bit of boiled linseed oil or other oil-based wood preservative. I would avoid insecticidal preservatives.

The newly constructed tray before sanding and staining is shown in **4–19**. Do not sand rough-sawn wood very much. Just touch up the edges and corners a bit to even out the joints and remove potential splinters. A too thorough sanding job makes the stain soak into the

4-12

4-13

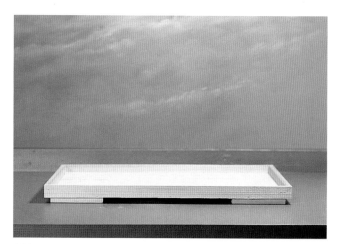

4-14

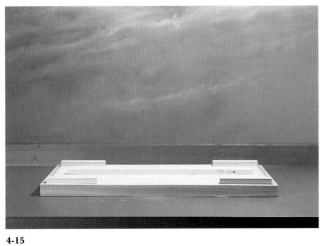

4-15

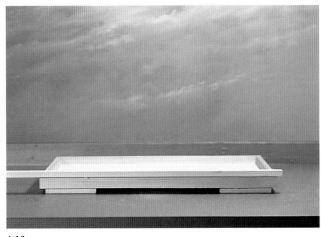

4-16

4-17

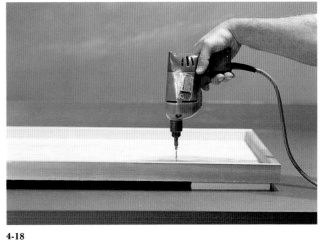

4-18

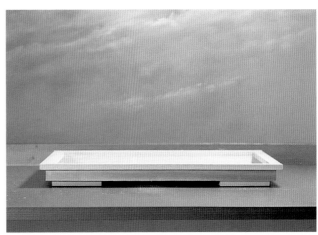

4-19

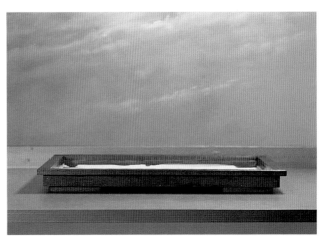

4-20

wood unevenly. The areas that have been well sanded will appear much lighter.

The completed tray ready for use is shown in **4–20**. One thick coat of Danish oil finish was allowed to soak into the wood for thirty minutes; then, with a rag moistened in mineral spirits, the excess was wiped off gently to keep the surface from drying sticky. An additional four hours of drying time made the tray dry to the touch. Make sure that you cover all surfaces that will show in the completed landscape planting—especially just inside the inner rim. A good arrangement of rocks and trees will show about one-half inch of the tray just inside the inner rim. Never build up the soil so that it is flush with the top of the tray. This makes the planting unsightly and difficult to water. You may choose to stain the entire container for added protection against moisture. I only covered the surfaces that I thought would be exposed.

BONSAI SOIL

I realize that it may be hard to imagine a soil that is especially suited for bonsai. Many people grow bonsai in ordinary potting soil with some degree of success. To make your job easier, however, I recommend trying a soil that is formulated especially for your plant. The Japanese bonsai soil-making screens shown in **4–21** are

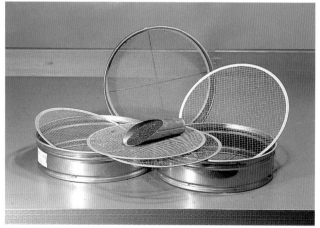

4-21

stainless steel, cost less than twenty dollars, and make foolproof soil that practically guarantees success. You can make your own screens as well, but I suspect you will spend more that way in the end.

The theory is this: soil particles smaller than one-sixteenth of an inch tend to compact and restrict air and water flow; so particles this size are removed. Soil particles larger than one-quarter of an inch are bulky and inefficient in a bonsai pot and they are removed as well. The procedure for making bonsai soil is simply to allow the soil to dry out so that it can be screened. Toss out all particles that will *not* pass through common hardware cloth or soffit screen; this is the large screen in the Japanese sieve. Then toss out all particles of soil that *will* pass through the smallest screen; ordinary window screen used to keep out insects in the summer will work well. The resulting pile of soil is the best potting soil on earth. (If it were not so labor-intensive, I would recommend it for your African violets, geraniums, and split-leaf philodendrons as well.) This is bonsai soil. It prevents overwatering, inhibits disease, and eliminates the concern about using salty or high-mineral-content water. Try it.

For very small pots, or for rock plantings, I recommend screening the soil slightly differently to preserve the smaller particles. Throw away all particles larger than one-eighth of an inch and do not discard anything smaller. Add 50 percent by volume shredded peat moss. Do not use the mossy, ropey kind used in wire baskets; rather, use the fine powdery type. Add 10 percent by volume bagged and processed steer manure (not right out of the field, please); then mix thoroughly with water until it resembles modelling clay. If the mixture continues to fall apart, you may have to add more manure. What you have just created is known affectionately in the bonsai world as "muck." This stuff will stick to anything. Use it for the creation of cliffs, ledges, and mountaintop plantings. Place your tree into a rock crevice and use this special soil to stick it there. Muck is nutritious and will not harm the plant. Additional air or drainage is not necessary due to the unusual location of the planting. This soil, in a normal-sized container, would turn to concrete, and it is not suitable for such use.

For additional holding power on cliffs or rock over-hangs, try a temporary net of string. The string will rot away in a year and the plant's roots will, by then, have a good hold on the rock. For stronger support, attach the string to a split-shot fishing weight, and then jam the lead shot into a rock crevice with a small screwdriver or nail set. The lead will conform to most cracks readily, and the string will still rot away. Avoid the use of copper wire, nylon netting, monofilament line, or other non-degradable supports. You would have to remove these nondegradable materials eventually, and, when you do, you disturb the planting and may have to start all over again. It is better to do it once, and then forget it. Plant your trees just once, and then watch the results grow.

The serious bonsai enthusiast has two bins full of screened soil particles waiting at all times. One of the bins contains 100 percent organic particles: bark, saw-dust, leaf mould, shavings, steer manure, or compost from the garden. Remember, "organic" means that it has been alive at one time or another; that's why it contains carbon. The other bin contains 100 percent inorganic particles, also screened. These might be decomposed granite, sharp sand, pumice, vermiculite, perlite, lava cinders, etc. These particles have never been alive, are high in mineral content, and high in pH.

The following soil-mixing guide may be helpful. Some of the major species are listed in five groups as examples to help guide you to correct soil mixing. These proportions are not extremely critical; they are in-cluded here as a guide to achieving an appropriate pH level in the soil. Particle size is actually more important than pH.

Group 1: ¾ Organic ¼ Inorganic
Azalea, rhododendron, bald cypress, redwood, tropical foliage plants.
Group 2: ⅔ Organic ⅓ Inorganic
Alder, birch, beech, hornbeam, elm, Zelkova, dog-wood, maple.
Group 3: ½ Organic ½ Inorganic
Pyracantha, wisteria, quince, fig, Corokia, holly, boxwood, apple, peach, pear, cherry, prune, plum, Cotoneaster.

Group 4: ⅓ Organic ⅔ Inorganic
Larch, ginkgo, fir, spruce, hemlock, cypress, Cryptomeria.
Group 5: ¼ Organic ¾ Inorganic
Oak, pine, juniper, alpine and desert plants, jade, Eucalyptus.

Fertile soil is never sterile. The word sterile, though, is sometimes used commercially to indicate weed-free; a bag of potting soil will often tout the word sterile as reassurance that the bag contains good stuff, not bad stuff. If the soil were really sterile, the contents would contain no living organisms of any kind. To say that the bag contains no life whatsoever is quite unlikely.

Many plants take advantage of microorganisms to accomplish life processes. Fertile soil is full of micro-organisms. Many forms of bacteria contribute to the breakdown of soil. The effects are quite beneficial and constitute what soil scientists call "ion exchange." All biochemical processes, when examined closely enough, amount to the exchange of positive and negative charges. Poor ion exchange means that there is a lack of important chemical interaction in the soil, which results in reduced plant performance. Avoid these pitfalls when selecting soil components.

Soil Components to Avoid

1. Any soil that does not have weeds growing in it.
2. Roadside soil, which may contain asphalt residues, pesticides, and dust that is difficult to wash out. There will be no beneficial bacteria.
3. Beach sand or soils. They contain salt and other minerals, and washing them out is inefficient and incomplete.
4. River sand. The edges have been polished smooth over time; there are no beneficial cracks and crevices for roots, moisture, nutrients, or helpful bacteria.
5. High-mineral soils usually collected in high-desert areas. Beware because these have often been formed as the result of sedimentation of alkali or brackish lake beds.
6. Discarded soil. It is tempting to reuse potting soil, but I cannot recommend it. Why didn't the former

plant do well? What was the former plant treated with in its lifetime? Perhaps nothing, but possibly insecticides, fungicides, nonutilized fertilizers, etc. It is best to start anew.

7. Used kitty litter. Even though you screen out the solid waste, the urine does not wash out easily or completely. The little blue or green particles in deodorized kitty litter contain dyes and fragrances that adversely affect soil performance.

Perhaps the most interesting microorganism in bonsai soil, or any soil, is mycorrhizae, a fungus. An extremely beneficial organism, it attaches itself to roots in the form of nodules that are quite visible to the naked eye. Their relationship to the plant is symbiotic. The mycorrhizae derives water and nutrients from the root, thereby eliminating the necessity for leaves. The plant benefits from the nodule because the fungus can process atmospheric nitrogen as a nutrient. For a high-altitude conifer, the benefit is especially appreciated. Nitrogenous compounds available as fertilizer to the windswept pine are all but absent. Whatever nutrition is available to the plant in this ecosystem is scarce, limited to infrequent bird droppings and the slow decay of a few needles that dropped from the tree. So this fungus is a beneficial organism that assists isolated trees in the wilderness. Your bonsai can also benefit from the existence of mycorrhizae if you inoculate your bonsai soil with a known population of the fungus.

When transplanting bonsai, I usually retain a bit of the old soil and transfer it along with the tree. For trees that are bare-rooted with water pressure in early spring, I retain a bit of old soil and add it to the new bonsai soils. When collecting trees from the woods, make sure you bring some well-rotted organic material along with the tree. It can come from around the tree itself, or simply find an established, mature tree of the same species, brush off the top layer of recently fallen needles and look for a slightly moist, partly rotted layer of needles below. This layer appears slightly frosted with beneficial moulds and fungi and has a characteristic rich, woodsy smell similar to Camembert rind. Dig up a couple of handfuls, making sure to include the top layer of soil as well. Keep this soil moist in a plastic

container until you're ready to plant your tree, then make a slurry, or suspension, of your mouldy needles by stirring them briskly in a bucket of water. Pour the container of water over the root area of your newly transplanted specimen. This technique benefits trees planted in the ground as well as trees planted in a container and can be applied to all species, not just pine.

Aesthetics

I like to think of bonsai as half horticulture and half art. That way of thinking serves me well when I want to stress the importance of a soil's color. From a purely horticultural standpoint, the tree doesn't care about the color of the soil from which it is growing. I must admit, however, my personal dissatisfaction with white-colored particles in some bonsai soils. There is something unsettling, rather cluttered and messy, about seeing perlite in bonsai soil. I find some pumices to be a bit better, but still quite obvious after a summer rain. Even vermiculite has rather crystalline flecks in its makeup, and similarly, red lava cinders are a distracting hue to my artistic sense. I find it disappointing to carefully choose a pot that complements the tree only to have the soil be a distracting element. Do not attempt to darken your soil with dyes because they are very salty. Over time, I have come to appreciate black lava cinders and decomposed dark rock as two superior inorganic soil components. They hold their color well, yet exhibit a wet–dry color change obvious enough to assist in setting watering schedules.

My favorite organic particle is hemlock bark, which, after having been aged for a year in the presence of steer or chicken manure, turns a dark, rich brown, almost black color. It holds its particle size for about five years, making it one of the best organic materials around for older potted specimens.

With all soils, the final test of a good soil is its performance with plant material. I highly recommend that you try to grow radishes in your prospective bonsai soil mix. Observe the radish plants carefully. A plant that

山光水秀 明川之

TOOLS AND EQUIPMENT

77

starts out with a flourish only to yellow, weaken, and become nonproductive will guide you as to what you need to add to your soil to keep your bonsai happy. A lush radish tip, but no vegetable, tells you that the soil lacks phosphorus and potassium. You need to nurture bonsai growing in this medium with 0-10-10 each winter. Look for chlorotic leaves. They can tell you that iron, sulfur, nitrogen, or trace minerals are lacking. Keep trying to grow that perfect radish. After all, if you can grow a radish in a bonsai pot, you will most likely succeed in growing miniature bonsai landscapes.

SAIKEI TRAYS

I have tried to give the reader affordable alternatives to imported ceramic, porcelain, and fired stoneware pots. The use of training pots and other alternatives works well for uncertain beginners in developing landscapes. Once you are ready to plant your miniature landscape in a beautiful finished pot, it is a glorious moment. The following containers represent a small sampling of what is available to the serious miniature landscape designer. They range in expense from fifty to about two hundred dollars, depending on size and quality.

The light brown-grey oval container in **4–22** is twenty-two inches long. It is ideal for a group of grey-barked alpine fir, grey-bark elm or similar-colored plant material. Its low rolled edge suits young plants as well.

The two fairly heavy trays in **4–23** do not have much room to create the illusion of extra depth. Use these for three rocks and five trees in a combination of rock planting and grove for best results.

The beautiful blue-glazed oval shown in **4–24** has no drain holes, indicating that it is a *sui-ban*, or water tray. Place a rock planting of maples on one side and fill the tray with water to make a reflecting lake.

Like the pot above, the *sui-ban* shown in **4–25** has no drainage. This container is more appropriate for a pine, spruce, or fir rock planting because of its earthy brown color.

The example shown in **4–26** is a truly magnificent

tray, and a difficult one to find. This *sui-ban* oval measures a grand thirty inches at its widest point and would make a rock planting of conifers look very special. There is even enough room for two or three islands.

The container shown in **4–27** is a heavier version of the saikei tray used later in Chapter Six. Its rim balances well with older plant material between five and fifteen years old. A landscape of five rocks and eleven conifers would look ideal in this large twenty-eight-inch tray.

The beautiful color of the glaze of the oval shown in **4–28** would complement most fruit trees. Try this twenty-four-inch oval with a grove of flowering almond, crab apple, or quince.

The smaller trays, ten and twelve inches across, shown in **4–29** make ideal containers for simple root-over-rock plantings. Train a trident maple's roots to grasp a good-looking stone, then place it on the blue-glazed tray. It will be spectacular.

The brick-red trays shown in **4–30** are the conifer equivalent of the above pots. For best results, plant with red-barked juniper, chinkapin trees, mulberry, myrtlewood, manzanita, or other red-barked trees.

A *sui-ban* the size of that shown in **4–31** needs an unusual-shaped compact rock to set it off. Try an eroded sandstone cliff with a windswept trio of rosemary plants for the look of an ancient Greek isle.

The unusual edge treatment of the fine blue container shown in **4–32** makes it the obvious choice for an elm, beech, birch, or hornbeam landscape. This pot is difficult to find, and its twenty-two-inch length makes it even more special.

It is hard to appreciate the container shown in **4–33** just from its photograph. It is an extremely well made sturdy saikei tray almost thirty inches across. Use a tray like this for that special old conifer planting. Your trees should have at least one-inch trunks to harmonize with this fine container.

The trio of pots shown in **4–34** can typically be found at most bonsai container outlets. They are great for miniature landscapes, rock plantings, raft plantings, or root-over-rock styles. Due to their color, they are most often used with broadleaf evergreens or conifers.

For strong upright spruce or fir groves, the angular rectangular pots shown in **4–35** are ideal. The largest measures sixteen inches across. Plant seven or nine formal upright junipers in these pots—the tallest plants with a nice *jin* at the apex.

I did not want to omit the plastic bonsai trays that now glut the market (see **4–36**). They offer a very inexpensive alternative for training or starting purposes. The sides of this pot are deep, making it nice for a raft-style juniper.

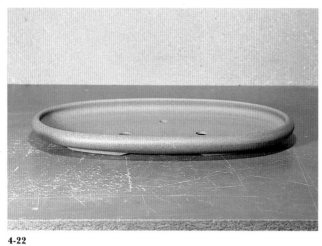

4-22

4-25

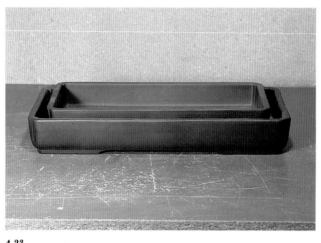

4-23

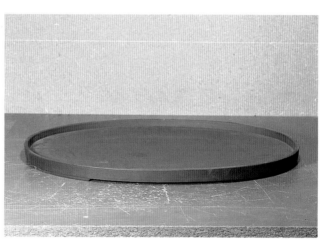

4-26

4-24

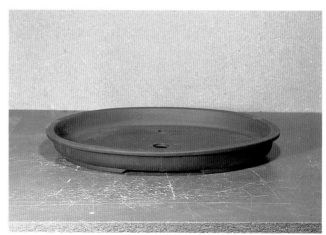

4-27

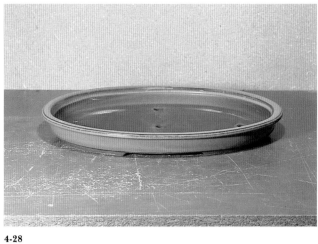

4-28

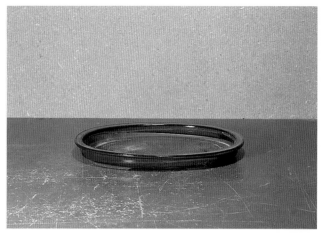

4-31

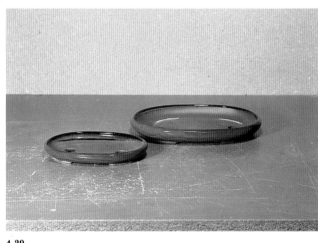

4-29

4-32

4-30

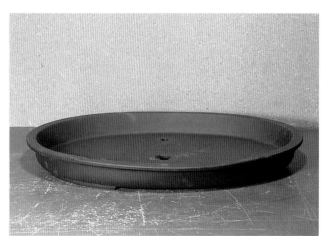

4-33

4-34

4-35

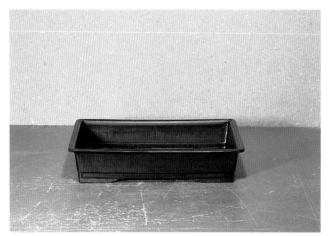

4-36

THE ART OF SAIKEI

82

5

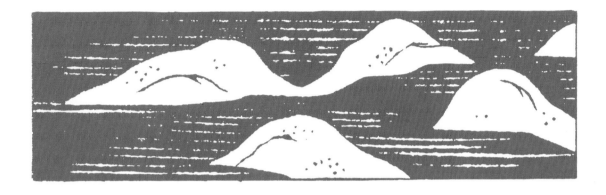

SAIKEI DESIGN AND DEVELOPMENT

ROCK STYLES

The Animal Stone

In order to assemble meaningful landscapes, it is best to know something about the shapes of rocks. Certain shapes resemble animals; others might look like houses, human figures, steps, waterfalls, mountains, and so forth. By grouping these styles of rocks, we can study how their shapes can best be utilized in the landscape. For example, the rock shown in **5–1** resembles a frog. It takes a bit of imagination to see the animal at first; but, after a while, the mind assembles a clearer picture. It is almost as if the stone begins the creative process and the imagination is left to fill in the details.

The frog is looking up at the sky. It seems, perhaps, as if a tasty fly is hovering nearby just out of reach. Look carefully, and you can start to make out the frog's right eye and the stretched amphibious skin at the base of its short neck.

This rock, by virtue of its resemblance to one of the many common creatures found in the landscape, becomes grouped as an animal stone. Once this classification is established, it becomes easier to place the rock in a landscape setting. It is true that the rock can be placed any number of ways; but only one aspect, or one presentation, is the best for this particular rock.

Let's look at some other view of the same rock (see **5–2**). The other side of this rock is quite uninteresting. The frog silhouette is retained, but the lack of detail on this side of the rock surface leaves too much for the imagination. It is too smooth.

Moving the rock to the right side of the container helps the presentation only slightly, as shown in **5–3**. The frog shape, by virtue of its having a head and a tail remnant, suggests direction by its placement, and it is far more comfortable having the head section overlooking the majority of the space contained by the boundaries of the pot. This phenomenon illustrates well how an outline shape suggests direction. Trees and rocks are similar in this regard. If a tree leans to the right, it looks best planted on the left and vice versa. As seen in **5–3**,

5-1

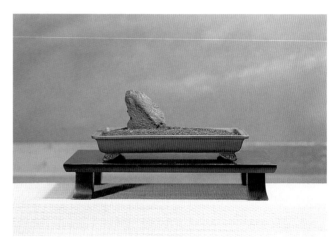

5-2

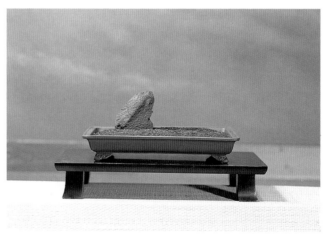

5-3

the slight lean of the rock towards the left makes it desirable to place the rock to the right side of the container.

If the rock is laid down flat on its side as in **5–4**, it immediately establishes an increase in visual stability. However, some inferior aspects can also be observed; it is difficult to tell where the top, or crown, is located. There is a certain roundness to the uppermost crown; but, when this particular area is positioned perfectly level, a distracting, almost horizontal line becomes noticeable just below. If the top is horizontal, this distracting line is not. Conversely, if this prominent line is adjusted level, then the top of the rock looks a bit crooked. In addition, a prominent vertical feature bisects the rock into even halves, an unnatural appearance. You will also notice that the rock is smaller at the ground level than slightly higher up, which tends to make the rock look "temporary." The rock appears perched upon the ground, which might evoke an unsettled feeling in the viewer.

By turning the rock upside down as shown in **5–5**, we can eliminate some of the problems posed by its former aspect. Notice that the rock "presents" itself well; it appears far more stable than before. The rock is now wider at the base than at the top, giving the viewer a message of permanence and strength. There is even a hint that we might be looking at only the tip of a much bigger rock. This optical illusion increases its sense of stability. The vertical feature so noticeable before is now less important because it is joined by other vertical lines to its left; the rock no longer appears evenly bisected. The crown, or top rounded area, is located slightly to the right of the rock's center of mass, which indicates that it will look better when placed on the right side of the pot.

Look carefully at **5–6**. Can you see the flop eared rabbit hiding in the landscape? Its left eye is the dominant dark area to the left. The uppermost crown becomes the spine. Its long legs are pulled forward, and the broad floppy ears that hang on the ground used to be just two ordinary vertical lines in the rock. The rock looks just fine in this position. Some rocks look well from many sides, and others look well from only one

5-4

5-5

5-6

SAIKEI DESIGN AND DEVELOPMENT

side. Still other rocks have no pleasing aspects *at all*, and should not be used in the landscape.

Rocks that are perfectly geometrical are difficult to incorporate with naturally shaped rocks and trees. Outline shapes of squares, rectangles, or circles suggest man-made objects and should be avoided. Egg shapes, triangles, and pyramids are also too "unnatural." A distant mountain may roughly resemble a pyramid or a cone, but the many imperfections on its surface make it a natural-looking phenomenon. Similarly, many boulders approximate rectangles, but their complex surface textures and rounded corners make them suitable for the landscape.

Let's consider some other aspects of our frog stone. Rocks or trees are always easier to assemble when there are an odd number of them; arranging two rocks is more difficult than one or three rocks. Let's give our frog two more companion stones (see **5-7**). A larger overhanging rock points in the same direction as the frog. The angles of both rocks complement and reiterate one another. The frog seems comfortable hiding under the protective shelter of the overhang as it gazes out over the third rock, which might suggest a lily pad.

Artistically arranging rocks, stones, or boulders requires thoughtful observation. By attaching additional significance to our stones, we can create meaningful plantings. Using our imagination we can assemble the individual elements into a whole that exceeds the sum of its parts. In addition, we each may derive a very real satisfaction or joy from being able to communicate to our viewers a short story, parable, or historic fable that is of some personal significance. Oriental gardens often symbolize struggles between perpetual adversaries or hint of some timeless legend. Why just plunk down a rock somewhere when you can elevate your art with simply a little more understanding? There will probably be some who scoff, but art is always for the beholder.

Ask any art teacher to explain how they teach art. Most probably the first step consists of learning and copying known, established techniques. As the student progresses, an experimental stage is reached where some basic rules are discarded. When, at last, the new artist has adopted an individual style—a signature of

5-7

sorts—the rules might be discarded completely.

Just for the sake of demonstration, let's try to assemble two companion stones with our frog. I am convinced that if the story doesn't make sense, the rocks will look random and haphazard. Let's face the frog towards a wall as shown in **5-8** instead of having it gaze out away from the wall.

The largest rock used to look stable and protective; now it appears precarious and threatening. I tried to duplicate the same angles as before to make a fair comparison. Many of the former lines and angles are repeated—normally a strengthening feature of a planting. Notice how the frog has lost its identity, and, therefore, charm, just because it now insists on staring into a rock wall. The "lily pad" on the right used to float on the pond. Now it appears that the pond has dried up and the small flat rock is all that is keeping the large boulder from toppling over.

The story no longer makes sense, and the planting becomes somewhat unstable and discomforting. What happens if we put the frog on top of the lily pad as shown in **5-9**? The result is not the ideal arrangement for these three rocks, but I think it demonstrates my point rather well. In spite of the awkward positioning of one rock directly on top of another, they look stable, calm, and meaningful. The frog is back to looking like a frog; and so the other stones look like a boulder and the lily pad.

The mind tries to sort out for us among the myriad

5-8

5-9

The Square Stone

The category of rock shown in **5–10** is characterized by square corners and a general bulky, geometrical shape. Its top is always presented horizontally, and one end of the rock should be tilted slightly towards the viewer. Real estate photographers favor this view of a house. Rather than present the flat front view of a home, a photograph that includes a slight glimpse of one of the sides as well gives the prospective buyer a better feeling of the depth of the structure. The same principle is effective with this shape of boulder. It is always rotated slightly to increase its depth.

Square stones seldom appear in the effective landscape alone. As you can see in **5–10**, by itself this rock presents a rather dull geometrical shape that cries out for the artist to break up its straight lines and surfaces.

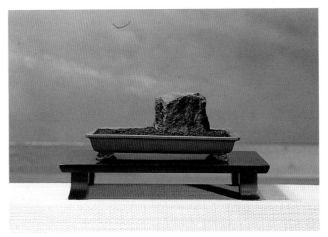

5-10

visual signals we receive, and, for some, it attempts to select those that constitute good art. We generally accept the input we receive as more or less random bits of information. If we see a beautiful tree in the woods, we might be inclined to take a photograph of it or draw it— or copy it as bonsai. Why did we not choose the tree right next to it? What was it about that particular tree that made it the object of our attention above all others? Surely the others have just as much right to represent nature's wonders. Oddly enough, it is likely that other people will notice the very same tree and have a need to reproduce it as well. In our effort to "improve" the tree, we will even circle it to search for its best side.

Let's explore this concept of "best side," using rocks in our miniature landscapes.

This is best accomplished with a couple of adjacent complementary stones. Notice how, in **5–11**, the adjacent stones break up the monotony of the sides of the square stone. The forward stone is not square. It, therefore, tends to soften the front surface and left edge of the larger stone behind it. The flat surface on the right of the square stone is similarly broken up by the appearance of the small stone in front of it. The three stones typify the most common arrangement found in oriental garden landscapes. The boulders might represent God,

5-11

5-12

5-13

Man, and Earth or possibly Man, Woman, and Child. The three stones are all different sizes, weights, masses, heights, and distances from each other. All three stones are viewed just off center in the container and rotated only enough to give the viewer a glimpse of their depth.

The Slanting Stone

The slanting stone, by its shape, placement, and composition as seen in **5–12**, suggests strong direction. If we view this stone upright as shown in **5–13**, it appears somewhat odd. The angled detail in the lower part of the stone seems strangely curved, and the top bump on the upper right sticks out like a sore thumb. A good slanting stone would be able to stand alone without support, either visual or actual.

A slanting stone points to an object of interest in the garden. Such a stone draws the eye in the direction of the slant to a stone of more importance. It is often found in gardens with a strong central focus, such as a waterfall, cliff, or pavilion. Trees planted nearby would typically slant in the same direction.

5-14

The Sentinel Stone

The sentinel stone is usually found standing alone as in **5–14**. They are large and imposing stones, representing legendary gods or warriors. If a garden depicts a story about Buddha, for instance, the boulder that represents his image is always a large sentinel stone.

The stone should sit comfortably on its own wide base. No feeling of instability should be perceived. The face of the rock should be well faceted and interesting, but not resemble a human face in any way. Smaller stones are displayed at a comfortable, "submissive" distance. Nearby stones, as mentioned above, are often slanted stones with their focus directed towards the sentinel's imposing presence.

5-15

The Distant Mountain Stone

Distant mountain stones, by their shape and placement, resemble a faraway peak as shown in **5–15**. They can get quite elaborate. An art form called *suiseki* elevates prized mountain stones into art for its own sake. In *suiseki* these natural stones are mounted on custom-made fancy wooden stands and used as "viewing stones," or as accompaniment plantings adjacent to bonsai. In the landscape—that is, saikei—however, they are positioned to take advantage of the depth that they can bring to a planting.

The distant mountain stone in the garden is designed to be viewed from one direction only. The stone does not have to be large and imposing to represent a mountain peak. With careful attention to placement, a rather small stone can suffice. Some of the most effective mountain stones contain quartz or other light-colored minerals that resemble snow from a distance. Observe how the same stone from **5–15** magically turns into a 14,000-foot peak when dusted with chalk and positioned between two modestly sized buttes as shown in **5–16**. It is *not* acceptable to physically alter the color of stones. I merely wanted to show you how just a suggestion of white on a rock can dramatically alter its appearance, and, therefore, its use in the landscape. Many rocks have naturally occurring crystalline streaks in them that evoke snow, whitewater, or surf. These valued stones can be saved for special uses in the landscape; they are very effective. By adding merely three small

5-16

5-17

driftwood snags in **5–17,** a complete landscape is formed. It is difficult in a photograph to communicate actual size, but to give you an idea of scale, the smallest dead snag is less than one-half inch high! This landscape can easily be held in one hand.

The Flat Stone

As the name suggests, flat stones are much wider than they are tall, as seen in **5–18.** As with most of the rock styles, it is best to use a stone that is slightly wider at ground level than at its top surface level. Position the stone so that some depth is achieved. This is accomplished by presenting a well-contoured, rounded, or faceted side—rather than one long boring edge as is the case in **5–19.** The flat stone in **5–19** might work better as a building block or for assembling a rock wall; but it definitely lacks the necessary character that would make it a candidate for a Japanese garden scene.

Flat stones are utilized as stands for stone lanterns, dish pools, bamboo knockers, or deer chasers. They make fine outcroppings into the edge of a pond—protruding from the shoreline as a decorative element in order to break up the monotonous curve of the shore. The flat stone can also, at the same time, function as a place to stand where the water is shady, and the view of the *koi* is better. When not in use by humans, the flat stone serves as a sunny, warm spot for the pond turtle to bask. In a cooler, more moist location, it serves as the nighttime perch from which the bullfrog can sing.

The flat stone perched on a pedestal in the center of the composition in **5–20** could serve as a natural seating place in the garden at the top of the stairs, or in a cozy spot where the view is particularly admirable. A water pump or an artesian spring could also convert this flat stone into an intimate waterfall.

5-18

5-19

5-20

The Stepped Stone

A bi-level "stepped" stone, as shown in **5–21**, functions in the garden as a transition stone. If a large boulder has an uninteresting face that needs hiding, the stepped stone softens the broadest and most boring of surfaces. This type of rock provides an ideal transition between sloping and flat ground. It serves equally well, both visually and functionally, not only to move the eye from the bank to the flat path, but also, to "become" actual steps. If it is the appropriate size and shape, the stepped stone can serve as the entryway into a teahouse or moon-viewing pavilion. Larger and more complex stones serve well as steps ascending into the home or up a sharp slope on the garden path. Stepped stones with only two levels can be further extended by utilizing flat stones and pedestal stones at either end.

To demonstrate one use of the stepped stone, we can set up a massive boulder as shown in **5–22** that has an uninteresting right side. We then insert a stepped stone as shown in **5–23**. Notice how the problem immediately disappears. Neither the stepped stone nor the large boulder could visually stand alone. Together, they are a welcome addition to the garden landscape.

The Overhanging Stone

Overhanging stones, such as the one in **5–24,** are hard to find and have limited value in the garden. Smaller versions make interesting pedestals for lanterns or bronze garden sculpture. Larger examples can create a dramatic water's edge. Perhaps the best examples, though, are very large boulders; they evoke cliffside images for cascading plants. Nothing is quite as dramatic as an overhanging stone with a weathered pine tree grasping its summit, one long branch hanging down from the edge of the cliff. The example in **5–24** is only slightly overhanging. Chinese *P'en Jing* utilizes rocks that are quite large on top compared to their tiny bases. It takes a bit of creative engineering to get the larger ones in place—and have them remain stable.

5-21

5-22

5-23

5-24

5-26

5-25

formed canyon is best "guarded" by a curved stone. When you look down the edges of two curved stones side by side, the horizon angles out of view, leaving the observer to imagine what is around the bend. This adds a further illusion of depth as well. If you form a miniature landscape where the end of the canyon can be plainly seen, your eyes are quickly bored. Create a gorge, path, or stream where the end is not visible because it gently curves out of sight, and the visual interest is greatly enhanced. Curving stones are useful elements in rock compositions. For the ambitious, a huge curved stone can make a natural bridge—a job for much heavy equipment—but it is occasionally done.

The Curved Stone

Curved stones can be quite interesting, as shown in **5–25**. They are utilized in the landscape for three purposes. First, they are the easiest way to enclose an area; a series of square, rectangular, or block stones often appear repetitive if lined up to form a wall-like barrier. A gently curving stone makes the transition from, say, north to east, in much more fluid fashion without the choppiness of a row of cubes. Second, the curved stone makes the most natural outside curve for a stream. When you look at **5–25,** it does not take much imagination to visualize a stream running deep at its vertical base; the shallow bank would, of course, be to the right of the pot. Third, the beginning, or entrance, to a water-

COMBINING THE NINE PRINCIPAL STYLES

These nine types of stones comprise the majority of the rocks suitable for creating landscapes, full size or miniature. Other shapes and styles, such as the basin stone, hut stone, figure stone, and chrysanthemum stone, are more appropriate as viewing stones, *suiseki,* or *P'en Jing.* For our purposes, therefore, let us concentrate on learning the interactions of these nine styles: the animal, square, slanting, sentinel, mountain, flat, stepped, overhanging, and curved stones. Let's assemble some simple combinations so that we can study how these basic nine interact with each other to create pleasing landscapes.

Three slanting stones are shown in **5–26**. An overhanging, stepped, and small square stone are combined in **5–27**. A large stepped stone is placed with smaller square and flat stones in **5–28**. Three curved stones form a composition in **5–29**. Three overhanging stones interact to form **5–30**. A sentinel, stepped, and flat stone combine in **5–31**. Three sentinel stones stand together in **5–32**. Two flat rocks and a distant mountain stone work together in **5–33**.

The reader may be surprised to know that all of the stones used to illustrate this chapter number only twelve. Most stones were able to do double duty. For example, one stone functions as a stepped stone from one side and as an overhanging stone when viewed upside down and backwards. These twelve stones were gathered in a matter of minutes from one source only: a small scree at the foot of the same exposed cliff of columnar basalt discussed in Chapter One and shown in **1–24**.

The important point I am trying to make here is that ordinary stones from your own locality will suffice in the creation of good miniature landscapes. Quality saikei come from the creativity of the mind, not the price of the raw materials. I think Toshio Kawamoto gave the world a tremendous art form; it is commonly available, inexpensive, and totally imaginative.

Years ago, a major American catalog retailer was promoting what was thought would become the ultimate business pastime. It was called the "Executive Sandbox." A small container of sand was poured into a shiny walnut frame secured with brass screws. Supposedly, the overworked, harried, and high-powered executive was to "play" in this box, alternately making and destroying personal creations. This creative outlet was touted to reduce stress by reverting to childhood activities and their associated fantasies.

Here is a better idea—and it won't cost you anything. Gather a bucket of beach sand, two handfuls of interestingly shaped rocks, and place them in a shallow container—a cookie sheet will do. Assemble and arrange these stones over and over into various landscapes. Challenge yourself to achieve the essential con-

5-27

5-28

5-29

5-30

5-33

5-31

5-32

tours found in natural landscapes that are meaningful to you. Do you have a favorite spot at the beach? How about trying to capture the feeling of a mountain stream? The Japanese feel that the topsoil surface of the earth represents the "skin" of the garden and the rocks form the "skeleton." Landscapes portray to the viewer essential and important structures—the lay of the land. At abrupt points of change, such as river bends and hilltops, the "bones" do not protrude, but they do stretch the outer skin thin to where their rocky shapes become quite obvious. In humans, this happens at the elbow, the kneecap, and the skull in similar fashion.

For a rock to show its form in the landscape without perforating the "skin" is the art of great stone placement. Anyone can plunk down a boulder in a garden. Integrating the rock with the form of the landscape takes thought and sensitivity. If the boulder protrudes too far, the scene appears as an "injury" or malformation. If the same boulder is buried too deeply in the topsoil, the landscape appears "flabby" and flaccid.

Let's study some of these rocks we have become so familiar with, but this time let us focus on two new concepts: first, the idea of forming myriad landscape forms with the same dozen rocks; second, observation of the location and depth of the surrounding topsoil to help us achieve a pleasant balance between "skin" and "bones" in the creation of a pleasing, natural landscape. For these studies, we should use a slightly larger container.

A traditional saikei tray is shown in **5–34**. This type of shallow dish has a small leading edge, and, therefore, does not obstruct the view or upset the scale of the trees or rocks planted within. Bonsai rules suggest that the height of the container be equal to the diameter of the largest tree found in the container. Obviously, when dealing with young seedlings whose diameters are pencil thin at best, this rule of thumb makes it difficult to select an appropriate container. The front edge of this saikei tray is quite thin, thereby complementing the narrow trunks of young plants. The oval pot measures twenty-two inches wide by seventeen inches in depth. The total height, including its short legs, is one and three-quarters of an inch.

Let's proceed with this study by considering simple design elements first and gradually progress to more complicated arrangements.

5-34

ONE ROCK

When one rock is positioned alone in a container, as in **5–35**, the rock itself must be of sufficient size and character to warrant the attention. It is much easier to mask ordinary stones when several are used in the planting. One ordinary stone alone in a large pot can make a weak statement. The stone in **5–35** is large enough to balance the container, but it does not have sufficient interest to

5-35

stand on its own. A rock somewhat similar to this might have sufficient visual impact to stand alone, perhaps, if it looked just like a thatched hut. This example requires just a little too much imagination. Therefore, this stone needs to be buried a bit in order to become united with its landscape.

The partially buried stone, as shown in **5–36,** appears to be a natural extension of the "hillside" around it. The topsoil is not completely flat and symmetrical around the base of the stone. Rainwater would flow off the surface of a great boulder. These rivulets of water, in a great downpour, would wash away adjacent topsoil in a predictable manner. When burying a stone of this size, it is important to observe such small details.

Notice the position of the rock in **5–36**. The top of the rock is not level. It is tilted so that the center of the exposed mass is located about one-third of the way from left to right. Notice also that the rock itself is positioned in the tray about one-third of the way from left to right.

The same rock has been overburied in **5–37**. The visual significance and importance of the boulder has been diminished greatly. At the same time, the surface area of the topsoil has been increased to where it is dominant. Great mounds of soil are not an imposing spectacle. If there is too much rock, the landscape appears injured, too angular—as if "broken bones" were protruding in a malevolent manner. If there is too much soil, the landscape appears overstuffed and inactive. The best landscapes display a good balance of both; the

5-36

5-37

throughout the book. Just as the Number One tree is always the tallest, the Number One stone is always the highest, regardless of mass. To number stones in order of decreasing mass is not always practical. Like an iceberg, much of the boulder is hidden or suggested by what is exposed, and massive rocks in the rear of a planting are not highly visible. In this planting, therefore, the Number One rock actually has less mass than rock Number Two. The additional rock is planted at a higher level than rock Number Two to provide interest. The additional height at the right of the landscape reverses the direction of the previous boulder. This makes it necessary to move them farther towards the right. The two rocks, when joined properly with topsoil "skin," form a single perceived rock mass. Notice that this combined mass is now located in the tray one-third of the way from right to left. Also, ignoring the soil and the container, the center of gravity of the rock is one-third of the way from right to left.

Perhaps we all have attempted to construct a mobile. We might have tried to balance seashells, balsa airplanes, cardboard cutouts, or holiday ornaments on long horizontal sticks. They would all be hung by thread so that the slightest breeze would rotate them. The trick was to attach the thread to each stick so that it could be moved and adjusted as additional weight was added.

Creating miniature landscapes is much like that process. The main "thread," the top long one that you tack

topsoil "skin" is displayed taut and vital, and its rock "skeleton" protrudes only where strong points in the structure make it necessary.

TWO ROCKS

The larger rock in **5–38** is the boulder from the preceding study. So that it is artistically pleasing as well as natural-looking, a second stone should not be the same size as the first. Considering the large size of the original stone, it was easiest to add a smaller stone rather than one even bigger.

Like trees in a group planting, stones can be numbered for ease of description. I use this designation

5-38

to the ceiling, is either one-third of the way from the left or one-third of the way from the right of your pot. Your task, as a landscape designer, is to visualize that every rock in that container is attached to a thin horizontal "stick" just as in the mobile. After all these elements are fastened, does the "stick" balance? Does it remain horizontal, or is it tilted down by too much visual weight on one side or the other? If so, you must make adjustments. You could move the objects along the "stick," add more objects to the light side of the "stick," or subtract objects from the heavy side.

Once your "stick" is horizontal and balanced, observe the direction of the planting. If it moves from right to left, center your top "thread" one-third of the way from right to left in your container. If the planting moves from left to right, center its total mass on the left side of the pot.

Let's state the above concept in a little different way, just to make sure it's clear. Imagine for the moment that you are a crane operator. You want to raise these two boulders out of the landscape simultaneously and without allowing them to rotate in any way. You would fasten a chain to the top of each rock above its exact center of weight. These two chains would be fastened straight up to a very strong horizontal metal beam. Now, the task is to calculate where to attach the crane to the beam so that when the rocks are lifted, they are lifted simultaneously and the beam remains horizontal. This is what I mean by center of mass. If the lift is successful, the tip of the crane will be positioned one-third of the way from the right side of this saikei tray. Look again at **5–38**, and study it for a while. Do you think the planting is balanced?

As you fashion landscapes, be aware of this concept of balance as you add elements. You will find that small rocks and trees have little effect on balance regardless of their location in the tray. Larger rocks and trees carry considerable "weight," and care must be taken during placement, particularly towards the edges of the container.

THREE ROCKS

The community in which I live has a butte directly to the south. Its upper surface has been eroded over time. In the summer, after a brisk four-hour hike, a spectacular view of the city is the reward. The planting shown in **5–39** reminds me of the summit of that butte. I can imagine myself sitting with my legs dangling over the edge of rock Number One, gazing out at the valley below.

The stone in **5–40** displays a nicely textured face, an attractively rounded crown, and a fine expansion near the soil line. But, it has some failings. One failing is a lack of depth. The protruding corner just left of center is not

5-39

5-40

sufficiently dominant to offer more than simple surface interest. Had it been more pronounced, this rock would be able to be displayed alone. As it is, we need to add more stones to the front and back in order to attain an adequate degree of depth. Another failing is the display of a "lower hem." A good buttress must appear progressively wider and wider at the base to give the stone visual support and stability. The lower edge displays a slight undercut at the right side and a marked indentation at its left edge. This rock is not buried deeply enough. It appears to have been deposited here, perhaps by a glacier, only "last week."

With the same rock buried properly, as shown in **5–41**, notice the added stability and apparent age. When the crown, or apex, is positioned in a well-balanced position, the right edge is nearly vertical and the left edge is slanting somewhat. This slight discrepancy creates a modest amount of movement in the stone, from left to right. Therefore, it is proper to place it on the left side of the pot. When we add other stones, we must be sure that these have the same direction and degree of movement.

When a second rock is added, three improvements to this planting are realized, as seen in **5–42**. The surface texture is matched and reiterated, which strengthens the visual statement made by the first stone. Had the additional stone displayed less or more surface texture, it would have appeared incongruous. (I have resisted the urge to display many "bad" examples of inferior plantings. My fear is that a browsing reader might mistake them for examples of what to do or, conversely, be horrified at what I appear to be "teaching.")

The single stone planting of **5–41** is also improved by the additional stone in **5–42** being positioned above and beyond the first. We achieve increased depth. Whereas the single stone looked lost in this large container, the pair of stones are able to make a substantial statement. Another improvement comes from the reinforcement and reiteration of the first stone. They both share equal degrees of movement from left to right. Their left sides mimic each other and their crowns are both roundly horizontal.

Moving on to three rocks, we can see in **5–43** what the

5-41

5-42

addition of one more stone does to the planting in **5–42**. The flat stone must be positioned behind the adjacent stone because, if it were placed in front, the three stones would be in a single line from left rear to right front. If you can always think in terms of an irregular triangle, you will avoid many pitfalls in design. Avoid straight lines and even geometrical forms. One key to good landscape design is the repetition of a single theme— but with subtle differences. Notice what these three rocks have in common: texture, color, direction, buttress, and crown. More important, perhaps, notice their differences: size, shape, mass, height, length, and position. Think for a moment about these similarities and differences.

The similarities are a function of our effort to maintain consistency, making sure that the natural history and geology of the stones are compatible. The differences derive from our inclination to compose the planting—to create art.

MATCHING ROCKS TO TREES

At this point, normal curiosity might ask the question "What kind of tree would I place in this or that landscape?" Answers should be starting to form in your mind. A suitable tree for **5–43** would have identical characteristics. It would form an irregular foliage triangle, wider than tall. It would have movement from left to right. The lowest branch would extend to reinforce the lines of the flat rock. It might be a mild windswept style or slanting style. It almost certainly would be a conifer in the barren landscape of **5–43**.

5-43

One Rock

The rock in **5–44** is not quite a distant mountain stone. It is more like a medium-close mountain stone; the Rock of Gibraltar, Citadel, and Yosemite's Half Dome all rolled into one imposing "2000-foot" protruding rock face. There is no need to bury this stone any further.

The task is to utilize such a dominant Number One rock, and then introduce other stones that will not detract. The large "water-formed" cut out on the rock's right side suggests that a small stream still bubbles along at its base.

5-44

Two Rocks

Rock Number Two can be added to the planting (see **5–45**). Remember our old friend, the overhanging rock? Here is an excellent opportunity to communicate the cumulative force of "water" that must have "carved" the lower face on rock Number One. The upward angle of rock Number Two reinforces and enhances the might of the peak and at the same time provides a logical explanation for the deep "water cut" below. It is easy to imagine an ancient stream passing along a crack between these two rocks. All that is necessary is time and this stream would reduce the surrounding landscape through simple erosion to expose the rock faces. Perhaps one might like to imagine a catastrophic event such as unprecedented glacial melt to widen the crevice if that helps visualizing a story in your mind; but actually, ordinary rainwater and rather tranquil stream erosion could carve this. In either case, common geologic history remains obvious, even after millions of years.

5-45

Three Rocks

Rock Number Three, hardly noticeable as added on the left of **5–46**, functions as closure. It turns the "stream" forward and defines the bottom edge of the peak. Notice how the soil buildup on both edges enhances the feeling of water in the middle. Landscapes have to make visual sense in order to feel comfortable. It is the "lay of the land" that is enough to suggest water. We have all seen artificial attempts at waterfalls, streams, and ponds that are not at all convincing precisely because they are overly literal. Water does not naturally tumble out of the top of a stack of rocks. Just presenting a strip of "beach" rock does not define a stream bed. A "pond" can be made by adding water to a doughnut-shaped hole lined with black plastic. These, however, are not pleasant, relaxing landscapes to gaze on—nor are they particularly convincing.

Trees

Before we leave the landscape that we have been developing in **5–44, 5–45,** and **5–46,** let's consider one more thing. What about trees? How big would they be in this planting? What type, variety, species, shape, and style would they have to be in order to complement what already has been assembled? I would suggest some small birch streamside on the right and some conifers on the left, something like what is shown in **5–47.**

Of the two Arctic birches found near the stream, the one on the left is just starting to show fall color, whereas the other is not. Since these birches were grown from seed, we can use their natural variation to our advantage. By planting the yellow one on the left, every fall, year after year, it will appear that sunlight is coming from the left side of this planting. Similarly, it would appear natural to have the dryer conifers on the sunny left side. The "southern" exposure on that slope would make it uninhabitable for any broadleaf evergreens. Furthermore, this orientation with respect to the sun

5-46

5-47

would account for the severe erosion of the cliff on the right, since that is the north face of the peak. Mountain climbers know that the steepest slope of most mountains in the Northern Hemisphere is found to the north. The freeze–thaw cycle is particularly severe, weathering rock faces especially by spalling off pieces in addition to the rock's ordinary chemical decomposition. The presence of a moving stream would contribute to the process and provide an avenue for removing weathered material.

Our composition is now total. We have a blend of rock, topsoil, moss, small ferns, ground cover, and deciduous and evergreen trees. We are not doing bonsai any longer; this is saikei. Some say it leaves less to the imagination than other bonsai-related art forms. I don't know. But I do know that, on a hot August day, I can "walk around" those two birch trees and on down to the pebbly shore. From there, my rod can throw a green nymph across to where an eighteen-inch brown trout sways gently against the deep, slow current in the shade of that mountain peak. Who says it's all in your imagination?

DEVELOPING THE COMPOSITION INTO A SAIKEI

I mentioned earlier that only a dozen rocks have been utilized for these demonstrations. Let's carry this idea one step further. Using the same stones—ordinary stones, remember—let's create landscapes familiar to us all. It is easier to form a seacoast with rocks that already look like ocean cliffs. However, one of the exciting aspects of saikei is that you can utilize ordinary stones and young plant material to achieve extraordinary results. All it takes is attention to detail. You must forget that your container has boundaries only twenty-two inches apart. The vision of the landscaper is what makes the miniature landscape special. Without vision, the container only provides size boundaries for a simple grove. With vision, the tray supports and enhances one-half

mile of sandy shoreline, one-thousand-foot waterfalls, or forty miles of snowcapped peaks.

When I was first learning to carve wood, I could not figure out how to carve the hairs on a cat. I kept trying to detail every hair with fine-toothed instruments. The carving only got worse, appearing only to be all scratched up. The professor patiently advised me: "Hair is not just a collection of animal fibres, it is the basis of the animal's shape. Form the shape and you have formed the animal." This principle is especially true of the landscape. With the right vision as to contour and position, the landscape becomes an artistic union of the topsoil "skin" and the firmament below. *Form the shape and you have formed the animal.*

The Seacoast

By now you are probably recognizing some of my twelve stones as seen in **5–48**. Our familiar friend, the overhanging rock, forms rock Number One with a parade of distant mountain stones close behind forming the back of the bay. A lone rock becomes an island on the right, and some smaller square stones fill in the hillside background between the cliffs. These latter stones provide depth and extra support to the ridge. Without them, the planting would become flaccid; the distant hills would look like huge stored piles of dirt in the back of the cliffs.

5-48

Can you visualize the types and sizes of vegetation that would complement this type of planting? Some windswept cypress in the foreground would look nice—perhaps even a solitary tree on the island. The distant mountains could be covered with a hairy-type moss to resemble a dense "pine forest," three miles distant. Some colored sand and gravel might be enough to suggest the ocean.

The Big Valley

The scene in **5–49** could be found in any number of places in the United States such as eastern Washington, the Appalachians, Utah, Nevada, or Wyoming. A large valley formed over eons comes to an abrupt end. The source of this river is a series of higher-altitude creeks converging at the base of the distant mountains. The ocean is behind the viewer. More snowy peaks can be found over the next ridge. On the Oregon Trail in summer, we might be just west of Fort Rock. If it were winter, we would be looking back at the mountains we had just traversed, relieved that we were now safely back down to 3000 feet above sea level.

This landscape would need some sage, thistle, and low-lying bear berry. A thin ribbon of gravel might define the location of the stream's trickling whitewater.

5-49

The Water-Formed Canyon

A few miles behind the rock wall seen in **5–50** lies a large, high-altitude basin that provides a constant flow of snow melt. The persistent water flow over this, perhaps, volcanic ridge which runs left to right has etched several small chasms in weak areas between outcrops. If we walked this ridge, we could view some of the other chasms.

The high force of the water flow in spring has left little topsoil. The vegetation that remains might be tall stately groves of spruce. Closer in to the water, a few aspen lean towards the light. Moss and lichen abound in the heavy damp air and at night, perhaps, a raccoon family emerges from its den on the left.

5-50

The Coastal Stream

As you can see, the scene represented in **5–51** will depend heavily on the foliage to complete it. Tall, dappled alder groves on each side of the brook might shade wild huckleberry and sword ferns. In actual scale, these trees would be ten to twelve inches tall. This saikei could easily accommodate fifteen deciduous trees. Birch, beech, hornbeam, Zelkova, and Chinese elm would serve as well as the alder. The only evergreens found in a grove of this type would consist of low, dwarf bushes of rhododendron or azalea. A conifer would be out of place. Again, plenty of moss would finish the scene quite nicely.

The purpose of the foregoing landscape designs is simply to illustrate how the shape of the land communicates the ideas. It is not the particular color or type of stone that is important; beaches are not made from "beach rock" any more than granite cliffs need be made of granite. A basalt rock can form a sedimentary ledge as easily as quartz can imitate a distant volcano. To be sure, some rocks lend themselves to certain applications better than others; but I hope you have seen that these twelve stones have successfully elucidated a variety of scenes quite competently. Success in saikei lies in the eye of the artist, the assembler of rocks and soil. A few seedlings finish the diorama. In your hands, a stone can form a ledge, a palm-sized slab can turn into a plain— and *rock becomes mountain*.

5-51

6

CREATING
A SAIKEI

The next logical step for us is to match trees to rocks. Typically we tend to do the opposite. At its most elemental, saikei may consist of one tree and a complementary rock. We will try some of these simple plantings and then progress to more complex and detailed living miniature landscapes.

ROCKY PLATEAU

The modest-sized pine bonsai shown in **6–1** is a *Pinus mugho mughus* "Green Candle." I have heard it stated among Japanese bonsai masters that if your tree requires elements such as rocks, ground cover, or shrubbery to evoke its environment, you have not designed your bonsai adequately. The tree alone should provide the viewer with enough information for imagining its surrounding landscape without additional trappings. On the other hand, saikei provides us with an opportunity to reinforce our ideas with these so-called trappings and extend those ideas to the viewer.

The tree in **6–1** is a fine example of an extreme slanting style, or *shakan*. Its heavy lean from left to right would earn it the qualifying adjective "extreme," or *dai-shakan*. What does this tree tell us about its environment? This is not a windswept tree because the lowest branch on the left seems too comfortable pointing straight towards the wind. This would have to be a tree found in a rocky area as evidenced by the strong root spread. It is probably surviving on a modestly elevated rocky plateau. Annual snow load accounts for its branches being horizontal even though this is a tree that has not reached its first "century" mark. We can tell it is not shaded by adjacent trees because the foliage is well distributed.

Analyzing a tree in this way helps us visualize the "landscape" surrounding the bonsai. Without such a description, would you have visualized so detailed an environment? You might not have. Even with the most careful observation, many of the details about a bonsai's surrounding environment are difficult to perceive. The miniature living bonsai landscape allows us an approach that, while not too literal, provides clues by

which we can fill in the blanks. We can not only suggest the tree's surroundings by means of the tree itself, but we can actually assemble them. Some may think that knowing more about a tree might limit the imagination; but I feel quite the opposite is true. The increased knowledge itself raises more questions and curiosity than answers.

6-1

Let us provide this small bonsai with an appropriate landscape. The tree is taken out of its container and planted one-third of the way from the left side in our saikei tray (see **6–2**). Obviously it is now quite "overpotted." The balance between plant and container is not appropriate; but, in creating our design, we expect that the increased mass due to the addition of rock will help tip the scales back into harmony.

Before we assemble appropriate stones, I will offer one bad example. I don't like to do this lest someone see the example out of context and mistakenly assume I am advocating such poor design; but, how often have we seen an incongruous rock plunked right down at the base of a bonsai? The rock shown in **6–3** is the wrong color, shape, size, type, and height. It detracts in every way from the landscape we seek. (I resisted the urge to place a small Buddha figurine here, as well, or include

6-2

6-3

an assortment of polished agates or petrified wood.)

The design shown in **6–4** is the rocky plateau that complements our tree. Notice the color, shape, and texture of the boulders. Their angles reinforce the lines found on the tree. This moss is the bright, shiny grey-green type found growing in full sun. The tree's roots reach out as if to grasp an unseen rock buried directly below. This must be September because the pine needles are fully opened—the next year's shoots are still small—and the fall crocus is blooming at the base of the

ledge on the right.

Does the presence of these stones restrict the imagination? I don't think so. In analyzing the simple potted bonsai that we started with in **6–1,** I had to work a bit to conjure up the appropriate landscape. With these vagaries solidified in the saikei of **6–4,** the landscape is represented in great detail. We can now concentrate on "looking for" the elusive ground squirrel and "listening for" the cracking sound the cones make when the autumn sun expands their seed casings.

6-4

CREATING A SAIKEI

107

6-6

6-5

THE OUTCROPPING

If you are at all familiar with bonsai, you are probably well aware that cascade-style bonsai, as shown in **6–5,** are planted in a tall container to accommodate the lowest branch which plunges downwards below the root buttress. Many of us have never questioned why, however. The cascade style exists in nature due to the way air currents behave. Glider pilots know that air "bunches up" next to vertical outcroppings. Above these landscape features, they can get an upward thrust of air that will give them additional altitude. The air that is congested directly alongside the vertical wall, however, is almost still. This stiller air relative to more harsh mountain winds favors the development of new growth.

Spring buds just popping out are subject to desiccation far more than their mature counterparts last year's growth. New buds predominate and thrive where the air is still next to the rock and expire in areas where the transpiration and desiccation rate is too high. The lowest dominant branch is not bent downwards due to the wind's "forces." It simply grows close to the surface of the rock because farther out it is impossible to survive.

Using the tree from **6–5,** let's imagine a story that harmonizes with the new saikei planting shown in **6–6.** One hundred years ago, say, at the top of the outcropping in **6–6,** an eagle's nest lay vacant. The young had all grown up and were making their own nests some distance away. Among the bird droppings, a solitary pine nut survived. Fueled by the heat of the sun and the nutrition of the guano, the seedling thrived—protected by the straw of the decomposing nest. Year after year, the buds that were able to survive the harsh seasonal changes shaped the tree into its present form. The tree clings close to the rock, almost as if to mimic the outline of the outcropping. Its only moisture comes from deep within the rock where the taproots seek out the last remaining water from the spring thaw. Its only fertilizer comes when a young eaglet returns for a moment and perches on the top of the tree. The eaglet is there because the pine is somehow familiar.

Just for those who might think these landscape creations are simply two-dimensional staging, I offer the view shown in **6–7** of the right side of this planting. This is definitely the edge of the planting, but it is still pleasing in all aspects. The tree remains balanced on its rock formation.

6-7

6-8

The stream effect is achieved by combining various colors of aquarium gravel. For wet effects, you can obtain the type of decorative gravel that is coated slightly to make it look polished. The coating makes the rocks particularly brilliant under grow lights or black light. If you are the adventurous type, I suggest you try viewing your miniature landscape sometime under black light indoors. It is quite a sight! The rocks, trees, and stream gravel take on a magical appearance right out of the "Legend of Sleepy Hollow."

NATURE'S HARDSHIPS

Imagine, one hundred and twenty years ago, that a small pine seedling, *Pinus contorta* 'Murrayana,' started to grow in a crack in a large boulder (see **6–10**). Some years were mild, but it seemed that most winters were too cold and summers too hot. The tree changed directions many times, but no one direction had any advantage. This is high country where some juniper is found—3500 feet above sea level. The tree's branches are pulled down sharply from the weight of five months' snow load each year. Time marches on slowly in this landscape; but some continuity is provided by the two-year-old pine seedling sprouting in the meagre shadow of the venerable old tree. Perhaps its offspring will have a less difficult time.

The view shown in **6–8** is from the rear of the landscape. The tree curves away from the viewer, reinforcing the concept of front versus back. The rock mass still balances the planting well. Normally you would not attempt to view a saikei from all angles, but I thought that it would be instructive to show these views. Miniature landscapes are not like store fronts or the set of a Western movie. They are real in every respect.

OVERLOOKING THE STREAM

The small grove shown in **6–9**—of trident maple, *Acer burgerianum*—was inspired by viewing the alder and cottonwood groves along the Columbia River near the Oregon town of Multnomah. The basalt cliffs at the base of the gorge have been severely eroded by ancient glacial activity. The banks are steep, high, rocky, and jagged, and the calm compositions of deciduous groves perched high above the water contrast sharply with the area's past geological history. This area is particularly spectacular in fall color—just as in this example.

BROOKSIDE

A low-altitude planting reminiscent of valley streams that trickle into a larger tributary is shown in **6–11**. The trees display the fall color of English hedge maple, *Acer campestre*. The twisted trunks and exposed roots tell the viewer that this area is subject to occasional flooding. But now, the area is calm with "Indian summer." The unseasonable dryness has reduced the bubbling stream to a mere rivulet—but still sufficient to provide a welcome drink for the deer at dusk.

6-9

THE ART OF SAIKEI

6-11

CREATING A SAIKEI

113

6-12

STREAMSIDE GROVE

The river winds its way along the left side of the planting of red maple, *Acer rubrum*, shown in **6–12**. Ferns, wild flowers, and mushrooms dot the trail that leads to this fishing hole. Just on the back side of this gentle knoll, the stream turns back again to the left. A large overhanging log lets me cast into the deep, clear pool below. On a good day, the alternating rushes of cool and hot air rustle the maple leaves above. On a great day, a spring steelhead trout finds my hook.

The container is a blue *Tokoname* ware oval saikei tray, eighteen inches at its widest point. The streamside pebbles are washed stream grit from the McKenzie river. The river color is from two shades of blue aquarium gravel highlighted with an occasional bit of chicken grit.

OLD GROWTH

Seldom do you see a quadruple-trunked tree in bonsai (see **6–13**). This three-tree grove of Alberta spruce, *Picea glauca* 'Conica,' has six apices due to the unusual four-trunked tree on the left. A variety of small bulbs bloom at various times of the year and the sword ferns thrive in the shade of these forty-inch, thirty-year-old trees.

6-13

SHELTER CAVE

The unusually shaped Mexican lava rock gives the saikei shown in **6–14** its cave. The ground cover consists of Corsican mint, blue star creeper, and Irish moss. Seven spruce, *Picea glauca* 'Conica Waconda,' stand sentinel over the shelter. The planting is eighteen years old.

6-14

THE ART OF SAIKEI

116

6-15

LAVA BEAR CAVE

A solitary spruce, *Picea abies* 'Mucronata,' guards the entrance to the animal shelter seen in **6–15**. Along the edge of the lava flow are plentiful huckleberry, salal, salmonberry, and wild strawberry.

6-16

6-17

NATURAL BRIDGE

The group of stones seen in **6–16** were collected from a weathered lava flow in Mexico. These rocks were favored when compared to the others in a great pile for the following reasons: their color was varied and interesting; the grain, texture, and direction of each of the five rocks were similar—in fact, two of these rocks were formed by breaking a larger stone in two: last, these stones had breaks that were not too obvious to the eye; there were fractures and jagged areas to be sure, but none were artificial in their appearance. Let's use these to assemble a natural-bridge landscape in a thirty-two-inch saikei tray.

Once the rocks have been assembled into a suitable arrangement, such as **6–17**, the next question practically asks itself. What size, type, and style of foliage would complement this landscape? I tend to lean towards a drier foliage, as seen in **6–18**. While there are possibly some natural bridges in wet climates, the best-known examples come from the high-desert country.

Natural Bridge National Park in the Western United States most vividly comes to mind for me.

One aspect of this miniature landscape we cannot possibly deny or overlook is that this "bridge" was originally formed by water erosion—perhaps where entrenched meanders on either side removed material and then breached the wall between them to form a new stream channel beneath the "bridge." It would seem obvious that we need to form the remnants of a stream bed under this dominant rock formation. To this end, we can sculpt a natural depression that continues under the bridge and fill it slightly with a matching colored gravel.

Close-ups of how the bridge abutments are secured to adjoining stones to give the feeling of naturalness and stability are shown in **6–19** and **6–20**. Juniper trees are planted in the rock crevices just where moisture becomes trapped. The rest of the landscape should remain relatively barren of vegetation. A lone aspen grows next to the water's edge.

6-19

6-20

CREATING A SAIKEI

119

6-18

CHINESE *P'EN JING*

We have, perhaps, seen some of the landscapes called *P'en Jing* in a bonsai magazine or in one of the recently published books on the subject. A classic book titled *Man Lung Artistic Pot Plants*, published in 1969 by the Wing Lung Bank, Hong Kong, might be one of the first glimpses that the Western world had of this unusual style. The Japanese landscape style might be characterized by striving to reduce visual input to its bare essentials. The Chinese tend to add just a touch of fantasy to their scenes. The *Literati* school of painting illustrated this tendency quite graphically. If a cliff was high, the vision of the cliff was subtly altered so that it appeared even taller, steeper, and more treacherous. Rocks were repositioned to appear very angular and dominant. Ledges were represented as precarious. The landscape scenes took on an air of a dream world, seemingly too rugged for life to exist. Thus, the startling presence of a hanging pine tree or a thatched hut became remarkable.

I include an example of this vast and complex Chinese style not to represent this single example as all-encompassing, but, rather, because I feel all saikei students should be aware of the existence of *P'en Jing*. Mr. Wu Yee-Sun, whose work appears in the aforementioned book, was one of my professors in China. Out of respect for the complexity of *P'en Jing* and Mr. Wu's work, though, I feel more comfortable limiting this discussion to this example and referring the reader to more specialized texts on the subject.

The stones that I selected for this planting came from a masonry supply. A stack of rock had been dumped from a truck between two concrete dividers. Surface nicks, scratches, and chips are obvious in the Number One rock seen in **6–21**. A light coat of linseed oil helps cover these abrasions. Notice in **6–22** how the many imperfections and surface abrasions are now covered up. The stone takes on a nice lustre and dark color. The angles become more pronounced and important. *P'en Jing* relies heavily on shape, angle, drama, and exaggeration; so the oil is helping to bring out these qualities in the rock. Traditional viewing stones, *suiseki*, are oiled

6-21

6-22

by rubbing them for years with the hands. Body oils slowly accumulate as the owner learns every nook and cranny of the stone. Applying boiled linseed oil is a much faster application of the same principle.

The completed rock formation is shown in **6–23**. Notice how the overstated landscape possesses power and fantasy as compared to the more subtle Japanese approach. The slight right-to-left angle is repeated consistently. Ledges for foliage are encouraged. Wherever possible, a stable buttress is displayed. The landscape is a bit monolithic, but inviting; this is not Stonehenge or Easter Island. While this scene could possibly exist in other worlds, its form is not entirely alien; it does not give one a sense of foreboding. When we view Chinese landscapes, we see a place that contrasts from our daily lives. We escape for a moment from the ordinary and travel to a place to which only our minds can take us.

Some simple trees and shrubs in **6–24** add to the fantasy of this miniature landscape. I have added three rhododendron, one pine, and two juniper. The complete absence of moss or ground cover suggests the notion that, sometimes, this can be a totally inhospitable place. A sea-green gravel has been added to represent water. There are no whitecaps, and there is only a slight breeze. Some *P'en Jing* artists would float a miniature wooden Chinese junk on the sea.

6-23

6-24

DESERT ARROYO

When water from a sudden downpour collects in the shallow valley in **6–25,** the stream-bed pebbles churn together. Vegetation is uprooted, and passage over the instant river is impossible. Once the area dries up, the polished stones appear disarmingly innocent and tranquil. About ten days later, the desert blooms. The *Haworthia* and *Opuntia* produce tall stalks of blossom. The sage opens its pale white flowers. The *Euphorbia* pushes out symmetrical rows of bright green leaves.

The miniature desert landscape has to be one of the easiest to create and maintain. These rocks are quartz from a local quarry. The smallest rock is critical for achieving the illusion of depth. This miniature landscape can be grown easily on a kitchen windowsill or patio shelf. The cacti really do bloom. Notice how few plants it takes to create an effective planting. We all have seen dish gardens and so-called cactus landscapes thrown together by local florist shops. Isn't this idea more effective and satisfying? I have to enjoy at least one story in every planting, however; did you notice the coyote den at the base of rock Number One? He is not home right now. He is out trying to catch a roadrunner.

6-25

6-26

6-27

THE UNICORN GARDEN

The three large rhododendron, *Rhododendron impeditum*, shown in **6–26**, will make up the bulk of this planting. I am inspired by Prof. Kawamoto's famous "Ancient Garden" planting, in which he utilizes Ezo spruce as focus trees. In the United States' Pacific Northwest, the native rhododendron, nurtured by mild climate, copious winter rain, and moderate summer humidity, grows high and grand. Old specimens approach the dignity of California live oak or the mature Chinese rhododendron stands in panda country. My object is to present the concept that large broadleaf evergreens can function as focal trees in a climax forest, not to imitate Prof. Kawamoto's work. We usually see these genera as smaller members under a tall coniferous grove; fir, spruce, or hemlock normally provide the necessary shade for the rhododendron to thrive. In more humid climates, mature rhododendrons achieve spectacular height, width, and trunk diameter. Trying to avoid Kawamoto's words "Ancient Garden," I searched for my own; my daughter, Aleta, has a favorite "animal," the unicorn. This seemed to portray the magical place I wanted to create: a place that is mysterious, but when you enter it, you have the odd feeling of having been there before, the pleasant, settling sensation of déjà vu.

The partially trimmed rhododendrons are seen in **6–27**. I have made an effort to remove crossing branches, old seed casings, dead twigs, and errant long water sprouts. These are remarkable trees. They are eighteen years old, in four-gallon containers. The trunks are an inch and a half in diameter. The roots are spread out and well developed. After cursory pruning, the largest tree was found to have trunk movement from right to left. Therefore, it will be placed in the foreground on the right side of the container next to the Number One rock.

The rhododendron outline shapes seen in **6–28** recall the California live oak. Mature groves of rhododendron resemble myrtle, magnolia, or the East African sausage tree. In spring, these trees will be covered with deep violet blooms. Below are planted *Rhododendron satsuki azaleas* 'Chinzan' and 'Shakusan.' The flowers are blue star creeper. Terrestrial and rock mosses and dwarf ferns complete the landscape.

6-28

6-29

6-30

Two close-ups of these fine rhododendrons are seen in **6–29** and **6–30**, which show that they could just as well stand on their own as bonsai. In the landscape I think they are more effective, however. The close proximity of the rocks, moss, and adjacent azaleas provide a scale and realism that cannot be duplicated in a bonsai pot. I wish with all my heart that bonsai teachers and students alike could appreciate all specimens of plant life. I say this with all honesty and certainty; if I were to take one of these fine rhododendrons to a so-called expert to work on at a local bonsai workshop, it most likely would be destroyed. I would return home with an embattled shrub in my hands, this fine plant reduced to a few meager twigs in an effort to make it look like a timberline juniper. It may "grow back out in time," but that is little consolation; we need to appreciate the full range of landscapes available to us—the rain forest and the stately old-growth forest—not just a few favorites into which we force beautiful plant specimens to conform, to their peril.

6-31

ANCIENT GORGE

The stream that runs between the formidable "cliffs" seen in **6–31** has created this crevasse and reduced the surrounding topography through the persistent wearing away by simple weathering processes of rain and runoff. But even with torrential flow during the Ice Ages the processes have been unable to reduce these monoliths to the same extent as the rock materials around them. Columnar basalt is a very dense igneous rock that is extremely resistant to erosion. Significant action on the cliffs is the freeze–thaw cycle, which works along the well-developed vertical fractures in the rock. A minimum amount of topsoil has been added in **6–31** (mainly to eliminate the appearance of plywood). Let's make this "moonscape" terrestrial by adding topsoil, moss, bushes, trees, and a stream bed.

I am sure you recognize in **6–32** the Number One rock from the previous *P'en Jing* landscape. Actually, these are all the same rocks. They have just been assembled differently. The taller trees are Alaskan red cedar, the medium conifers are *arborvitae*. The smallest are *andelyensis* cypress. One would not actually find these species together in the woods. They are used to achieve a greater degree of scale than can be achieved by using one type of tree alone. *Arborvitae* has the advantage of appearing in miniature to resemble full-grown cedar at a distance. The tight, compact foliage of *Chamaecyparis thyoides andelyensis* 'Conica' looks like cedar at an even greater distance. The slight trickle of "water" is formed by banks of brown and grey pebbles with a center "stream" made of two shades of blue gravel that is dotted occasionally with white to resemble gurgling whitewater. Caution is advised when using colored gravel or sand; a little goes a long way. Pay close attention to the scale of the surroundings. Overstatement becomes garish and tacky. Remember, from the previous chapter, "the shape makes the animal." Water does not have to be represented by water; cedars do not have to be cedar.

6-32

6-33

6-34

SANDSTONE SHORELINE

The three lava stones seen in **6–33** will make up the bulk of the planting. They were selected for their interesting caverns and convolutions. In not too distant geologic time, the Pacific Ocean was lapping against the western edge of the Rocky Mountains. At one time parts of the terrain that now includes the states of Washington, Oregon, Idaho, California, and Nevada were completely under water, did not exist in any recognizable form, or were somewhere in the vicinity of Australia or New Zealand, yet to be "rafted" across the then Pacific by means of plate tectonics, misnomered as "continental drift." Seashell fossils are now found in much of western North America from Alaska to Mexico. Minerals or grains that make up rocks tend to align with the magnetic field of the earth at the time they were formed. Measurements of this "remnant" magnetism places some rocks that are now in western North America on the other side of the earth when they were formed. But, through the action of the shifting of the earth's plates and volcanic activity, the Pacific Ocean is now located about two thousand miles west of where it once was. I find it somehow profound and appropriate to use these volcanic rocks from western Colorado to form this sea-shore. It makes me wonder, Could these very three stones have actually tasted the salt of the Pacific Ocean at one time?

The stones are more or less in place in **6–34**. Some adjustments may be necessary in order to incorporate the plant material. These rocks are most interesting because, in this position, their tops are dark. If the shoreline is reversed so that the ocean is to the right, the stones would have to be turned upside down in order to maintain the illusion of depth. The present dark tops would then be buried in the soil, and the light tops would be exposed, an almost white sandstone reminiscent of the Greek Isles.

Somehow, this planting just had to have windswept cypress as seen in **6–35**, recalling Pebble Beach and the Monterey Peninsula in California. The "Pacific Ocean" is formed here by rust-colored pebbles at the shore, teal gravel, and white gravel waves. A darker patch of blue indicates where the water is deep and you can "dive for abalone." Between the smallest two rocks, a stream enters the sea from the nearby Coast Range.

The combination of moss, water, and muck enable the landscape designer to form steep yet stable cliffs of vegetation (see **6–36**). I refer you to Chapter Four for the recipe to make bonsai muck.

6-36

6-35

6-37

ROOT-OVER-ROCK MAPLE

An interesting rock planting can be made by combining three trees to make one tree, as in **6–37**. Three Japanese maples are stripped of their lower leaves. Their long, slender trunks are inserted into the cracks and crevices of a suitable rock. This lava rock resembles a modest-sized cliff or ledge and has a few "passageways" where the thin, flexible trunks could be inserted. The three trees are tied together at the top of the stone with a loop of copper wire or several wraps of floral tape. After about one year, the three trees will meld together as one, and the wire or tape can be removed (see **6–38**). These trees are fastened together by a common layer of cambium. The "trunk" of the future bonsai landscape tree will swell up and form where the original trees were fastened together. This planting is only eight months old. The three trees have permanently joined together already. Now we can start training our future bonsai. The trunk will adhere to the apex of the lava rock. The "roots" will be formed from the old trunks of the three trees, and the branches will be trained as traditional bonsai.

6-38

OLDUVAI GORGE

Among the many sights I wished to see in my lifetime was the famous site where Dr. Louis Seymour Leakey had made such great contributions to anthropology. It is with considerable pride and respect that I attempt to reconstruct the excitement and emotion associated with that landscape. The four stones that created the natural bridge seen earlier will form this ancient human site (see **6–39**).

The great Rift Valley of eastern Africa extends from southern Ethiopia through Kenya, Tanzania, to northern Mozambique. This geologic feature includes such natural phenomena as Ngorongoro Crater, the Serengeti Plain, and Mt. Kilimanjaro, the highest mountain in Africa. As an amateur anthropologist, I always wondered why or how Dr. Leakey could have selected this particular spot to rummage for remains of ancient human ancestors. One only has to visit the site to begin to surmise the logic. Why excavate when a very old stream has done most of the work for you? Every layer of reddish rock uncovered by the waters' actions unveils tens of thousands of years of history. Artifacts found at various layers might enable the entire strata to be bracketed by known archaeological dates.

The rocks in **6–40** were chosen for their reddish color that imitated the Serengeti and because they were horizontally layered, imitating the sedimentary layers of the Olduvai. The rocks are in place. Vegetation can be added now that reflects the arid conditions of this almost desert landscape.

The story of the landscape in **6–41** can now be "told." The thorn trees are lush after a November rain. This dry area no longer supports much wildlife. The secretary bird, the dik-dik, and the dung beetle are about all that remain. "Olduvai" means "lily" in the language of the local Masai tribe. At the edge of the stream we can start to see the annual emergence of this old form of plant life. In another three weeks of this austral spring, it will again bloom just as it did many thousands of years ago.

6-39

6-40

6-41

TIMBERLINE

For this planting, we will create an old timberline juniper by using a technique known as the "phoenix graft." The underlying theme in the legend of the phoenix, a mythical bird, is that "from death comes life." From the death of a juniper stump (see **6–42**), we can create a live juniper bonsai by fastening them together permanently. A young and supple *Juniperus horizontalis X media* 'Shimpaku' is chosen as the live portion of this "graft" because of its superior foliage (see **6–43**). It is a needle-type juniper with compact blue-green foliage that is not prickly to the touch. (This makes it a favorite juniper for those with sensitive skin or juniper allergies.)

We cut off all but one long leader on the juniper (see **6–44**). Select the most flexible leader and the one that most closely follows the contours of the driftwood stump (see **6–45**). Tracing the undulations of the live tree directly on the dead stump with a marking pen, as shown in **6–46,** we then can carve out a groove so that they fit together snugly. This can be accomplished with wood-carving tools, drills, a rotary tool, a die grinder, or even a chain saw. (*Extreme caution* is advised when working with the chain saw, however.)

Once the groove is established to the diameter of the juniper, cut off unneeded branches that interfere with insertion into the stump. Strip off a narrow band of bark from the side that will contact the inside of the groove. This will promote outward growth only. When the juniper is in place, firmly attach it to the stump with nails or small screws. Do not worry about the heads of the nails showing. The new bark will cover them over in a few years as the juniper grows. In time, one will not be able to tell the difference between the donor plant and the recipient stump. Old juniper always grows in long strips anyway. All you are doing is copying what would happen in nature over a long period of time.

Our finished timberline planting is shown in **6–47**. On the right is our phoenix graft on a high rocky ledge overlooking a barren valley. On the left is a medium-sized butte with accompanying foothills and young cedar trees. In the distance, a small range of snow-

6-42

6-43

6-44

6-46

6-45

CREATING A SAIKEI

143

6-47

6-48

6-50

6-49

6-51

6-52

capped peaks is formed by placing quartz stones with their pointed edges upwards. The largest snowcapped mountain you may recognize; it is the smallest quartz rock in the desert planting earlier in this chapter. It was simply repositioned so that one of its sharp points is aligned vertically instead of horizontally.

A close-up of our timberline, windswept juniper shows the exposed rootage and the construction of the rocky ledge (see **6–48**). The far-left basalt rock is our old friend the "frog" from the beginning of Chapter Five. We have come a long way.

The medium-distance scene is formed from familiar stones as well (see **6–49**). The dry stream bed is granite grit mixed with grey aquarium gravel to produce a slightly polished appearance.

A close-up view of the driftwood shows no scars from the chain saw or rotary tool (see **6–50**). The new foliage will fill out in time, but I think you can see that it will be quite easy to train the juniper down and along the dead branches. Even the new future top is well placed and directed. In time this plant will look stunning.

The trick to creating an effective distant-mountain appearance is to bury the inappropriate parts of the stone thoroughly (see **6–51**). Form ridges and undulations in the ground level for more interest and to create a more natural appearance. Mountains seldom rise straight out of flat ground, so utilize adjacent ridges,

foothills, and valleys. Make sure that your peak is just above the horizon. There is a tendency to try to make a mountain appear ridiculously high by having it be the tallest element in the pot. In this planting, notice that the snowcapped peaks are, in reality, the lowest rocks. This is always true when you gaze at distant mountains in nature.

Looking at **6–52,** is this a miniature bonsai landscape, or are you standing at timberline next to a twenty-foot-tall gnarled juniper looking out at a sixteen-thousand-foot-high peak forty miles away? This is the magic of saikei. The container is only sixteen inches deep, and with vision, imagination, and attention to detail you can have the wilderness on your kitchen window ledge.

My objective throughout this chapter has been to, in a sense, walk you through these examples to encourage and inspire you to try your own miniature landscape. With just a handful of stones, some immature plant material, and a generous dose of imagination you can create special places. By no means have all the possible landscapes been attempted here. Waterfalls, quiet glades, moors, and rolling hills have not been represented. What is your favorite? How would you go about constructing it? What plant materials would you use? What type and size of rocks? Answer these questions and you are on your way to an enjoyable experience with the art of saikei. Give it a try.

7

ANNUAL CARE

7-1

To demonstrate the steps necessary to ensure that your miniature landscape maintains its shape, vigor, and health, we will use the forest planting of Japanese larch shown in **7–1** as our subject. We will progress through the kinds of things that require annual attention. This larch grove is starting to show a nice golden fall color, and fall is an ideal time to prune and repot all trees. The fall colors indicate that the trees are just starting to go into dormancy for the winter. Any pruning, trimming, or work with the roots will be safe at this time of year. The weather will still be warm enough for two more months so that the trees can heal their wounds. In the spring, we will not have to disturb the trees; they will be trimmed and shaped already. Their established rootage will be anxious to reach out into the new soil provided. Spring is usually a busy time of the year for bonsai growers. It is good to know that the major work on this planting will already be completed. We can just add a bit of fresh fertilizer, stand back, and watch it grow. This grove is sitting on a turntable for easy access to the branches. Pruning must be done on all branches on all sides of all the trees.

PRUNING

The close-up of the right side of this planting in **7–2** shows us that late summer growth has become a bit crowded between trees and has sprawled out on the outside.

This growth must be directed in the proper direction by cutting branches back to a useful bud (see **7–3**). Next year's growth buds can already be seen this year as dark brown spots or swellings along the twigs. To direct next spring's growth, simply cut the branch back to a point where the end bud is pointing in a desirable direction. Do not trim a branch back to where its end bud faces straight up or straight down; in the spring, such new growth will just have to be cut off anyway. Trim now to avoid this redundancy.

The same area of the grove is shown in **7–4** after a few minutes of trimming. Notice that the ends of the branches are flattened a bit horizontally from upward and downward twig removal. The terminal buds are pointed horizontally and outward, as well, so that, as these buds break open next April, they will be pointing their new branches in the right direction, thereby saving a lot of work later on.

7-2

7-3

7-4

REPOTTING

Let's take this planting outside for repotting. This can be done inside with a spray bottle, but it is easier to accomplish outside with a hose-end sprayer.

The soil surface of this planting has a great deal of debris on it from early fall (see **7–5**). We can wash most of this away during repotting. The weeds seen in **7–6,** however, will have to be carefully dug out with a pair of tweezers or they will overwinter in the pot and come up even bigger in the spring.

With landscape plantings, it is not necessary to separate the individual trees (see **7–7**). After its first two years of growth, the miniature landscape's roots grab hold of all the available soil; even rocks in the container will feel their grasp. Very large rocks, such as what you might use as a mountain or cliff, may be successfully removed before repotting by carefully separating the plants from the stone. These plants can be reunited with the stone after fresh soil has been added.

7-5

7-6

7-7

Removing from the Pot

Remove the entire planting from the container. The roots of the plants will hold each tree in position exactly as before. The bottom surface of the combined rootball is shown in **7–8**. Notice where the drain holes used to be located. You can see where the root growth has been inhibited by the presence of the galvanized hardware cloth and the copper wire staples. Drainage in this container has been enhanced rather than reduced by covering the drain holes with these screens. Drain holes without this covering will become quickly clogged with root growth seeking air. They will congest towards the bottom openings in the pot and thereby reduce the flow of water through these important exits. The addition of copper wire staples to these protective galvanized screens not only prevents the entry of insects, but further inhibits root growth around the drain holes because of the chemical interaction of the copper and the iron. The lack of concentrated roots at the drain holes promotes continual good drainage between repottings.

The planting has been totally removed from the saikei tray in **7–9**. Smell the roots. If they have a noticeably rotten odor to them, it is better to leave the planting like this for several days. The smell of root rot is unmistakable. For years, I always wondered how it was that wine connoisseurs were able to detect an inferior bottle by smelling the cork. I guess you have to be served a bad

7-9

bottle to appreciate the poignancy of the moment. You do not have to get the wine anywhere near your lips, much less your palate. The cork comes out decomposed, soft, black, slippery, and rank. It is similar with potted plants. Notice the shiny white succulent root tips on the edges of this planting. They are your first indication of good health. If a planting has root rot, these white tips are small, dark, slippery, and smelly. The fragrance of healthy soil can be described as woodsy, earthy, and damp. Sometimes the smell reminds me of wild mushrooms or fresh potatoes in a bag. If you suspect root rot, treat the rootball with a fungicide and leave the planting just like this for a few days. Without the container, the roots can breathe more easily, and they will heal faster.

Cleaning and Root Pruning

Rinse the planting several times with fresh water to remove organic soil particles that have decomposed (see **7–10**). Inorganic soil particles maintain their texture and size from year to year. Products such as sawdust or fine bark chips decompose with bacterial action in less than a year. The smallest particles will turn to mush and will start to clog the interstitial spaces in the soil. A thorough rinsing during repotting will clean out the soil and flush this waste out of the way, restoring good drainage. By adjusting the spray on the watering hose, surface debris such as needles, mushrooms, leaf mould,

7-8

and scum can also be removed.

Work from the edges with a dull root hook, separating out clumps of roots (see **7–11**). The overall goal is to remove about 25 percent of the total root mass. As the roots are combed out, seek out congested root areas, and thin them out. Remove all muddy areas entirely, washing them clean. Turn the planting on its side, and loosen the tight roots that have formed a solid plate on the underside of the landscape planting.

When you have loosened up or removed approximately 25 percent of the existing roots and soil, scrape away any unneeded ground cover (see **7–12**). The landscape should be covered with no more than 50 percent mosses and ground covers immediately after repotting. These can be allowed to grow back to cover 80 percent of the soil surface over time, but removing most of them during repotting ensures that the roots will receive maximum air for healing.

Wash away all loose soil, roots, moss, ground cover, gravel, and surface debris in a final and thorough shower before adding fresh soil (see **7–13**). Wash the soil surface, all edges of the planting, and the underside of the combined rootball. Force the hose into crevices between trees and around rocks where present. Make this a fairly harsh watering session to rid the planting of a year or two of waste products and harmful mineral deposits.

Allow the washed planting to drain for one-half hour (see **7–14**). Tip the rootball on its side for a few minutes to make sure that excess water has drained out. If the effluent water is still dark or muddy, wash again with the hose. Continue flushing the planting until the drainage is clear; then let stand for another thirty minutes.

7-10

7-11

Preparing the Pot

Scrub out the container with a mild bleach solution to disinfect it (see **7–15**). Then, scrub with a mild detergent, such as a liquid dishwashing detergent, to remove all traces of bleach. If white mineral deposits persist along the inside rim of the pot, they can be removed with full-strength vinegar on an abrasive Teflon cleaning pad. Rinse well several times. Check for cracks; do not use a damaged pot. It will break easily during the winter and be responsible for drying out your planting. When the pot is totally clean and dry, I recommend that you mark it with your social security number or some other identification code on the inside with a diamond engraver or indelible permanent ink marker. In case of theft, this is a sure way to identify your planting in front of a police officer. It may not seem pleasant to bring up the possibility of someone stealing your planting, but if everyone used an identification code, bonsai theft would be severely curtailed.

Cut out new hardware cloth screens or soffit screens to replace the old screens in the pot (see **7–16**). Secure these screens with copper wire staples (see **7–17**). Add a fresh layer of bonsai soil to the bottom of the tray. Mix the soil according to the suggested proportions found at the end of Chapter Four. Each species of tree prefers a certain pH of soil; the guide found in Chapter Four will help you achieve the best mix for each type of plant.

Once the soil is in place, tamp it down slightly to make sure there are no air pockets in the edges or corners (see **7–18**). Dampen the soil slightly with a diluted mixture of vitamin B_1 in water at a dilution rate of one teaspoon per gallon of water. Vitamin B_1 helps new roots grow in the first few critical days after transplanting. Do *not* use this dilution on your plantings one week later; its effects will be minimal to none.

7-12

7-13

7-14

7-15

7-17

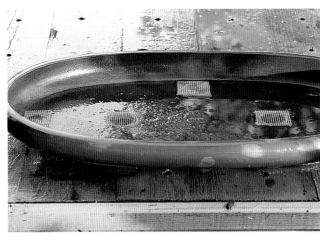

7-16

7-18

Replacing the Planting

Place the planting back into its container (see **7–19**). Wiggle it around a bit so that imperfections on the underside surface of the trees become stuffed with soil. Pack down gently with your hands all around the sides. Look carefully at the planting. Is it too low? Is it too high? Does it lean to one side? Is it centered in the container? Check the planting from all sides before adding any more bonsai soil. More soil may have to be added underneath to raise the planting to its ideal height. Some soil may have to be removed to preserve the illusion of a middle running stream or pathway. Make these adjustments now, before adding more soil. When you are satisfied with the final position in the pot, add a little bonsai soil at a time. A soil scoop will be very helpful.

Build up the soil all around the edges of the container and up into the planting where the hose has eroded away muddy areas and exposed tree roots (see **7–20**). Add excess soil now, making sure that all areas are well covered. Repair moss and shrubs as needed.

With a pair of chopsticks positioned as shown in **7–21**, fill air pockets under the new soil. Do not jamb or drive the sticks into the soil. Push the two sticks gently but firmly into a suspected air pocket, then rapidly vibrate the chopsticks from side to side to cause the dry soil particles to pour down the edges of the sticks and into the air pockets. Many students jab at the roots with heavy, aggressive, and damaging thrusts which are both unnecessary and hurtful to the remaining roots. A gentle thrust with both sticks in one hand while vibrating them rapidly accomplishes better results with less damage in half the time.

Add more soil as needed until no more bonsai soil can be incorporated; then sweep off the excess with a small brush or broom (see **7–22**). Contour the soil with the brush to allow for slopes and undulations in the landscape. Do not make it smooth.

Brush off all excess soil on the landscape surface, pot edge, and potting bench (see **7–23**). Study the ground contours, and make sure they are correct. With the fingertips or with a bonsai potting trowel, form a small quarter-inch rim just inside the edge of the container. This edge not only makes the planting look more finished, it helps prevent the accumulated buildup of excess minerals and salts in this area. It is also easier to water the planting when the soil does not come over the edge of the pot.

Compress depressed areas with your fingertips, making sure that these areas are in contact with the new soil below (see **7–24**). Replace gravel, rocks, stones, and other accessories as needed. Again, you will find that small scoops and tweezers will help get these items back into place where they should be.

The finished planting after repotting is shown in **7–25**. The gravel path is in place, weeds removed, moss cleaned up, wild flowers replanted, new soil added, and the land recontoured. Hearty fall growth will precede winter dormancy and a vigorous, healthy spring. Notice the proportion of ground cover to bare soil. The dark color of the pot and the bare soil combined will absorb heat from the sun during the next few weeks. This heat will promote some root growth and healing before winter arrives. A solid mat of moss would keep the soil too cool, thereby inhibiting fall growth and healing. Compare **7–25** with **7–5** to appreciate how much has been accomplished in about an hour.

Apply a light spray of vitamin B_1 solution, one teaspoon per gallon of water, to the new planting which will help the new roots get started (see **7–26**). Under *no circumstances* add fertilizer of any kind. Fertilizers will raise the osmotic pressure of the water and make moisture effectively unavailable to the newly cut roots. Do not fertilize for three weeks, then only sparingly with liquid 3-10-10 or similar.

7-19

7-22

7-20

7-23

7-21

7-24

7-25

7-26

Winter and Summer Care

The larch planting is returned to the growing bench as seen in **7–27**. It is a cedar platform forty inches above the ground. The slatted bench surface provides maximum drainage, yet displays the planting quite well. The cedar slatted sides and top are adjustable for the seasons. More slats are added for hot or windy days. As fall approaches and more sunlight can be tolerated by the plants inside, slats are slowly removed and redistributed. Some areas of the bench can be adjusted for more or less light than others. For instance, a section for pine and juniper might have no overhead protection at all; whereas a section containing Japanese maples may be half covered. As winter approaches, clear plastic sheeting can be added to the windy side. Eventually the entire structure is double-wrapped in clear plastic with ı layer of chicken wire fencing between layers for strength against possible strong gusts. A power extension cord runs from the house to the structure to supply electricity to a small space heater and three light bulbs that are placed on the ground underneath the shelf. A thermostat turns on the heat at 32 degrees Fahrenheit (zero degrees Celsius). I can tell if the thermostat is working by watching the light bulbs go off and on while I am enjoying the warmth and comfort of my dining room. I recommend three bulbs due to the high failure rate of light bulbs under these conditions of cold and moisture. There is enough of a backup so that your plantings are not placed in jeopardy. By the time the third bulb blows, it's time to check the bonsai anyway.

Before finishing with the repotting section, I feel it is necessary to stress the need for regular doses of water on the newly transplanted landscape (see **7–28**). Water twice daily for three days; then once daily for a week. After that, water when surface dryness appears, but no less than twice a week for the next month. Regular waterings as needed are sufficient after that. A light application of liquid fertilizer is useful after three weeks; but apply only diluted fertilizer to an already watered planting. Then wait thirty minutes, and water again with clear water to remove excess fertilizer.

7-27

7-28

WATERING

Working for a nursery in Japan, I was completing an apprenticeship. I was eager to be more involved beyond the weeding and general cleanup duties I had been given, and asked if I could help water. My professor told me quite matter-of-factly that the day I was allowed to water his bonsai would be the day I graduated. This statement took me by surprise; how was I supposed to learn how to water? Why wait so long? I was informed that the duties I had performed thus far were an opportunity for me to learn without the possibility of failure. When the time comes that I am invited to learn how to water, it would be an admission by the master that he was entrusting the life and death of his prized possessions to me. It was the last step of an apprenticeship, signifying "graduation." I did progress from weeding to moss removal, and eventually I was permitted to prune off a few errant twigs. One day I was finally handed the master's copper watering can. I accepted it with a great deal of pride, because I knew it was my diploma.

Watering is not a task to be taken lightly, for it is true: you have the power of life or death in your hands. How many of us have gone on vacation and arranged for our neighbor to water our houseplants? In just a week's time, disaster can happen. Actually, only two things can occur: overwatering or underwatering. Let's study each separately with an outline of proper watering technique in between.

Overwatering occurs, of course, when too much water is applied to the plant. Fortunately, there is an easy solution. If your bonsai soil is screened properly as suggested in Chapter Four, overwatering becomes nearly impossible. The screened soil particles will allow the excess water to immediately pass through the drain holes. Standing water is immediately removed by gravity alone.

Here is the best way to water. First, water the planting lightly; avoid using great quantities of water. The dry soil is not yet ready to receive the full benefits from this moisture. Wait ten minutes; walk away, water other plants, do some other chores, whatever, but walk away. During the ten minutes, the moisture in and around the container will have broken down the surface tension of the dry soil. Water will no longer be repulsed by the soil particles and will not bead up. The soil mass will have expanded slightly as well, thereby closing off the large air passages along the inside edges of the container. Most of the first, light watering will have passed rapidly through these large channels and failed to moisten the bulk of the root ball.

Now, with the second watering, apply a small but steady stream directly to the top of the container. Occasionally, a short, crisp blast of water is needed to knock off dust from the foliage; but, for the most part, avoid watering the foliage. The tree will be cleaner, free of moss and algae on the trunk. The planting will also be less apt to attract insects and disease if the foliage is kept dry. After the thorough second watering, again, leave the tree for ten more minutes.

In this next ten-minute period of rest, undissolved minerals and salts, fertilizer waste products, and tiny, muddy, organic soil particles will be emulsified or dissolved. They will be loosened from their attachments to the container, to the roots, and to the soil particles themselves. The third and final watering will cleanse the rootball thoroughly as the flush of water carries this waste down through the drain holes of the container. These three waterings are considered one "watering." Whenever you water, the definition of watering consists of these three separate steps. Leave out one or two of these steps and you are not really watering at all.

Water in the morning rather than evening. Plants that "go to bed" at night still wet are apt to get mildew and other related, more serious disease. If you must water several times a day in hot summer weather, make sure that you do not water the foliage. Also, make the last watering of the day no later than four o'clock so that the plant will be dry at nightfall. If you find you must water more often, you may have a pot that is too small, roots that are too root-bound, or a location that is too sunny. Check these conditions and make necessary adjustments.

Underwatering is usually caused by scheduling problems—such as vacations, long work days, hot weather, or just rushing through the watering process.

ANNUAL CARE

You might consider using hose timers; they are becoming less expensive every year as microchips become more common. Every garden supply has at least two or three to choose from; some are battery operated, some operate mechanically like an old-fashioned egg timer. Still others are hard-wired to the home's electrical circuits and may need special plumbing as well. These timers can control a hose-end sprinkler, an underground sprinkler system, an overhead misting system, or a small-tubed drip system which dispenses water directly into the container. If you have difficulty keeping your bonsai or miniature landscapes moist, consider looking into one of the many watering systems available. Design and use the method most appropriate for your physical layout and personal schedule. A word of caution here: all systems fail at some time or other, and some fail more often than others. Plan on a way to double-check your watering system often, or you could be disappointed some day.

FERTILIZERS AND FERTILIZING

If you have ever noticed, all products that are sold as fertilizers, or that are reputed to supply nutrition to plants, are required to have three numbers affixed to the label. This is the NPK designation—for nitrogen (N), phosphorus (P), and potassium (K). A bottle that claims to be a 3-10-5 fertilizer, for instance, contains 3 percent nitrogen, 10 percent phosphorus, and 5 percent potassium. Most bonsai prefer living at about a 3 percent nitrogen level in the soil. More nitrogen and the leaves grow too big. Less and the leaves become too yellow. By choosing a liquid fertilizer, you can easily dilute it in your watering can with a minimum of stirring. Application is then safe when the diluted fertilizer is added to an already moist bonsai. Never fertilize a potted plant when it is dry.

Choose fertilizer that has a nitrogen value that tends to be slightly lower than its phosphorus and potassium levels. Numbers such as 10-15-10, 5-10-10, and 3-10-5 are common. Remember that if you double the suggested volume of water, you halve the percentage values of the nutrients. A 10-15-10 fertilizer might suggest 10 drops of this fertilizer into a quart of water. If you put the 10 drops of fertilizer into a half gallon of water, you have created a 5-7.5-5 fertilizer—a good one for bonsai.

Normally, potted plants need small doses of nutrition every two weeks while they are actively growing. Avoid fertilizer in extremely hot weather or in the winter. Look at the leaf color for the best biological indicator of need. A leaf with green veins and a yellowish background needs nutrition. If nitrogen does not help, try a bit of iron as well. If the leaves are big, full, and very green do not fertilize for several weeks. Wait until a slight yellowing becomes visible, otherwise an excess of fertilizer residues may build up in the soil. Pine trees and other conifers will display the same yellowing with a single green midrib on the underside of the needle. You may need the help of a magnifying glass to observe this clearly.

INSECTS

Fortunately, bonsai and miniature landscapes are, of course, smaller than their full-sized counterparts in the backyard and the woods. Most pests can be picked off with a pair of tweezers. There is no point in mixing up a quart of insecticide for a ten-inch tree that has two caterpillars on it. In general, your bonsai will be as healthy as your surrounding garden. If you have a known infestation of tent caterpillars, for instance, every May in your weeping willow, take care of the larger problem, and your bonsai will take care of themselves.

Aphids are by far the most common pests of bonsai worldwide. Fortunately, their eradication is simple. They are an extremely soft-bodied sucking insect that is susceptible to detergents of any kind. Gently add one teaspoon of liquid dishwashing detergent to a quart-sized plastic spray bottle filled with lukewarm water. Do not shake, but rock the bottle back and forth, until the soap is in solution. Spray the bonsai just to the point of wetness, not dripping wet. Cover in particular new growth and the undersides of leaves. Repeat every three

days until the aphids are gone, then spray once more.

Scale insects are a problem on most trees and shrubs. They appear as immobile brown spots on succulent growth. Soak a cotton swab with vegetable oil and cover their crusty shields with oil to suffocate them.

Whitefly is a persistent pest that commonly invades greenhouses and sunny, still locations. The plant, when touched, will exhibit a sudden exit of tiny white flecks that resettle quickly back onto adjacent plants. This is a tough pest to cure; but the placement of yellow sticky traps around plants seems to keep the problem under control. Your local garden centers handles these traps.

The woolly aphid resembles a bit of cotton that has somehow stuck to a leaf or needle. It doesn't seem to be an insect at all; but watch how it can multiply. The simple detergent that works for the common aphid will work for the woolly aphid also, but you must add a sticker spreader to the solution. This product is available at most garden supply stores.

Considering the wide variety of insects throughout the world, it would be foolish to try to discuss all possible pests. For questions and problems in your area, consult local nurseries, landscape companies, garden clubs, or government agricultural inspectors.

DISEASES

Luckily, most plant diseases are preventable by taking precautions in and around the growing bench. Clean up all rotting debris from your trees' foliage, containers, benches, under the pots and around the area. When you trim off a suspicious-looking withered branch or mouldy leaf, sterilize your tools before moving on to prune a healthy tree. A light swabbing with rubbing—or isopropyl—alcohol is sufficient sterilization. At the first sign of powdery mildew or fungus infection, treat the area with a reliable fungicide. Avoid watering on moist, warm, humid days. Avoid wetting foliage at any time. Throw away—do not mulch—diseased plants. They should be hauled away or incinerated. Avoid growing bonsai under disease-susceptible trees—such as peach, dogwood, pear, apricot, or citrus. Avoid growing bonsai near rose bushes, blackberries, grapes, raspberries, or tomatoes. Avoid problem areas under known diseased shade trees or trees which constantly shed sticky residues or other debris. Once every summer clean off your bonsai bench with soap and water; then spray a strong bleach solution, and let dry. On deciduous trees always use a dormant spray of lime sulfur or copper to eliminate overwintering insects and disease. This is an inexpensive, nontoxic solution that cures most pest problems. Put this application into your annual schedule; do not forget. It is well worth it.

MYSTERY PROBLEMS

As my concluding thoughts on our exploration of the art of saikei, I would like to leave you with two main points. First, when in doubt, check with an expert. There are countless numbers of qualified people and agencies in your area that are willing to help identify a problem and suggest a solution. Get a second opinion, if you feel it is warranted. Do not just hope that the problem will go away on its own, and wind up doing nothing. Often, it gets worse. I don't want to recount the number of times I have been asked to "treat" a tree that had died two months prior to my seeing it for the first time.

Second, in case of emergency, take your tree out of the pot and plant it in the ground. This simple solution will take care of overwatering, underwatering, toxic levels of pesticides, minor insect infestations, most diseases, dehydration, and sun scald. Do not hesitate! Minutes count! Take the tree out of the pot, and plant it just as you would a shrub. Water it well, and leave it alone until it looks better, even if that takes two years.

In closing, I hope by now that you have already been enjoying creating your own miniature living landscapes. Part of the satisfaction is that you can quickly compose and disassemble landscapes or preserve a particular planting for years. Another part of the satisfaction comes from knowing that, in your hands, a few seedlings turn into old-growth forest, a bit of colored gravel forms an ocean, and rock becomes mountain. It is in this expression of our vision and the story we create for our miniature plantings that saikei becomes an art form. My best advice to you is to keep it simple and imaginative. Plant your landscapes to satisfy yourself—that is most important—and you will also please most of the people most of the time. I hope you have gotten as much enjoyment as I have, not only making the plantings in this book, but with the ongoing learning process as well. This endeavor has been a personal one. Thank you Professor Kawamoto. I think the rock, for me, has finally become a mountain.

Appendices

Suggested Saikei Sources

PLANT MATERIALS LIST

This plant list is quite extensive, but by no means complete. Utilize native materials whenever possible. The seeds of plants from your own region sprout easily in the soil. Use cuttings as necessary when specific cultivars are choice and rare. Do not use grafted stock; it is not only unnecessary, but rather ugly as well. Miniature living bonsai landscapes thrive on the use of common, everyday materials, both plants and stones.

Acer palmatum, *Japanese maple*

Abies amabilis	Silver fir
Abies balsamea 'Nana'	Dwarf balsam fir
Abies koreana	Korean fir
Abies lasiocarpa	Alpine fir
Abies lasiocarpa 'Arizonica'	Cork fir
Acer buergerianum	Trident maple
Acer campestre	Hedge maple
Acer campestre 'Compacta'	Compact-hedge maple
Acer capillipes	Japanese red maple
Acer circinatum	Vine maple
Acer ginnala	Amur maple
Acer griseum	Paper-bark maple
Acer japonicum	Fullmoon maple
Acer japonicum 'Aconitifolium'	Laceleaf fullmoon maple
Acer japonicum 'Aureum'	Golden fullmoon maple
Acer oblongum	Evergreen maple
Acer palmatum	Japanese maple
Acer palmatum 'Arakawa'	
Acer palmatum 'Butterfly'	Japanese butterfly maple

Acer palmatum, *Japanese maple "Waterfall."*

Acer palmatum 'Kiyo Hime'	
Acer palmatum 'Koshimino'	Dwarf Japanese maple
Acer palmatum 'Linearilobum'	Thread-leafed maple
Acer palmatum 'Sango Kaku'	Coral-barked maple
Acer palmatum 'Shishigashira'	
Acer paxii	Lobed evergreen maple
Acer rubrum	Red maple
Acer saccarinum grandidentatum	Rock Mountain maple
Acer tataricum	Tatarian maple
Acer truncatum	Chinese maple

Acer palmatum dissectum *"Garnet," Japanese maple.*

Acer palmatum, *Japanese maple "Shojo Shidare."*

Acer palmatum, *Japanese maple* "Beni-Hime."

Acer palmatum, *Japanese maple* "Otto's dissectum."

Acer palmatum, *Japanese maple* "Viridis."

Acer palmatum, *Japanese maple* "Shishigashira."

Acer palmatum, *Japanese maple "Beni Maico."*

Camelia vernalis	Vernalis camellia
Carpinus betula	European hornbeam
Carpinus caroliniana	American hornbeam
Carpinus turczaninovii	Turkish hornbeam
Cedrus brevifolia	Cyprian cedar
Cedrus libani	Cedar of Lebanon
Cedrus libani 'Nana'	Dwarf cedar of Lebanon
Celtis sinensis	Chinese hackberry
Cercis chinensis	Chinese redbud
Cercocarpus ledifolius	Curl-leaf mountain mahogany

Albizia julibrissin, *Mimosa or silk tree.*

Albizia julibrissin	Mimosa or silk tree
Alnus tenuifolia	Mountain alder
Arctostaphylos manzanita	Manzanita
Arundinaria disticha	Dwarf fernleaf bamboo
Arundinaria marmorea	Dwarf black bamboo
Betula 'Nana'	Dwarf Arctic birch
Betula pendula 'Fastigiata'	Pyramidal white birch
Betula pendula 'Laciniata'	Cutleaf weeping birch
Betula pendula 'Purpurea'	Purple birch
Betula pendula 'Trost's Dwarf'	Trosts dwarf birch
Betula platyphylla 'Japonica'	Japanese white birch
Buxus microphylla 'Compacta'	Dwarf boxwood
Buxus microphylla 'Koreana'	Korean boxwood
Buxus microphylla 'Morris Midget'	
Calocedrus decurrens	Incense cedar
Camelia sasanqua	Sasanqua camellia
Camelia sinensis	Tea

Cedrus deodora pendulum, *Weeping Deodora cedar.*

Chaenomeles japonica	Japanese flowering quince	*Chamaecyparis pisifera* 'Filifera'	Threadbranch cypress
Chamaecyparis lawsoniana 'Ellwoodii Improved'	Ellwood cypress	*Chamaecyparis thyoides andelyensis* 'Conica'	*Andelyensis conica* cypress
Chamaecyparis lawsoniana 'Minima Glauca'	Dwarf blue cypress	*Chrysanthemum morifolium*	Chrysanthemum
Chamaecyparis nootkatensis 'Compacta'	Dwarf Alaska yellow cedar	*Citrus*	*Nagami* kumquat
		Clematis montana	Anemone clematis
Chamaecyparis obtusa 'Filicoides'	Fernspray cypress	*Coffea arabica*	Coffee
		Cornus kousa	Korean dogwood
Chamaecyparis obtusa 'Kosteri'	Koster cypress	*Cornus mas*	Cornelian cherry
Chamaecyparis obtusa 'Nana'	Dwarf *Hinoki* cypress	*Corokia cotoneaster*	Corokia
		Corylus avellana 'Contorta'	Harry Lauder's walking stick
Chamaecyparis pisifera	*Sawara* cypress		
		Corylus colurna	Turkish hazelnut
		Corylus maxima 'Purpurea'	Purple filbert
		Cotoneaster congestus	Congested cotoneaster
		Cotoneaster microphyllus thymifolius	Thyme-leaf cotoneaster
		Crassula argentea 'Crosby's Dwarf'	Dwarf jade
		Crassula tetragona	Succulent pine
		Crataegus ambigua	Russian hawthorn
		Cryptomeria japonica 'Bandai-sugi'	Conical cryptomeria
		Cryptomeria japonica 'Jundai-sugi'	Globular cryptomeria
		Cryptomeria japonica 'Pygmaea'	Dwarf cryptomeria
		Cryptomeria japonica 'Tansu'	*Tansu* cryptomeria
		Cupressus forbesii	Telcate cypress
		Cupressus macrolarpa	Monterey cypress
		Eurya emorginata microphylla	Japanese fern tree
		Fagus sylvatica 'Asplenifolia'	Cut-leaf beech
		Fagus sylvatica 'Atropurpurea'	Copper beech
		Fagus sylvatica 'Lanciniata'	Laceleaf beech
		Fagus sylvatica 'Rohanii'	Oak leaf beech
		Fagus sylvatica 'Spaethiana'	Purple beech
		Fagus sylvatica 'Tricolor'	Tricolor beech
		Fagus sylvatica 'Zlatia'	Golden beech
		Fuchsia 'Isis'	Fuchsia
		Grevillea rosmarinifolia	Rosemary tree
		Hakonechloa macra 'Aureola'	Japanese forest grass
		Hamamelis mollis	Chinese witch hazel

Chamaecyparis obtusa *"Meroke," Hinoki cypress.*

Ilex crenata 'Mariesii'	Dwarf Japanese holly
Ilex dimorphophylla	Okinawan holly
Imperata cylindrica 'Rubra'	Japanese blood grass
Juniperus chinensis 'Parsonii'	Prostrate juniper
Juniperus chinensis procumbens 'Nana'	Japanese green mound juniper
Juniperus chinensis 'Sargentii'	*Shimpaku*
Juniperus chinensis 'Blaauw'	Blue *Shimpaku*
Juniperus chinensis 'Torulosa'	Hollywood juniper
Juniperus chinensis 'Skyrocket'	Skyrocket juniper
Juniperus communis compressa	Dwarf columnar juniper

Juniperus procumbens nana, *Japanese green mound juniper.*

Juniperus X Media *"Shimpaku,"* Shimpaku *Juniper.*

Juniperus squamata *"Blue Star,"* Blue Star juniper.

Larix decidua	European larch
Larix kaempferi	Japanese larch
Magnolia parviflora	*Oyama* magnolia
Malus 'Dorothea'	Yellow crabapple pink flowers
Malus floribunda	Japanese flowering crabapple
Malus 'Radiant'	Red crabapple red flowers
Malus zumi calocarpa	Red crabapple white flowers

Juniperus horizontalis *"Wiltoni," Wiltoni juniper.*

Myrtus communis 'Microphylla'	Dwarf myrtle
Narcissus 'Minimus'	Dwarf daffodil
Narcissus 'Triandrus'	Angel tear daffodil
Nothofagus antarctica	Antarctic beech
Olea europaea 'Little Ollie'	Dwarf olive
Parrotia persica	Persian beech
Phoenix roebelenii	Pygmy date palm
Picea abies 'Mucronata'	Dwarf spruce
Picea abies 'Pygmaea'	Pygmy spruce
Picea engelmannii	Engelmann spruce
Picea glauca 'Conica'	Dwarf Alberta spruce

Picea orientalis *"Gracilis nana," Dwarf Oriental spruce.*

Larix decidua pendula, *Weeping larch.*

Picea orientalis *"Repens," Oriental spruce.*

Picea sitchensis, *Sitka spruce.*

Pieris japonica 'Compacta'	Dwarf andromeda
Pinus albicaulis	Whitebark pine
Pinus aristata	Bristlecone pine
Pinus balfouriana	Foxtail pine
Pinus bungeana	Lacebark pine
Pinus cembroides monophylla	Blue Piñon pine
Pinus contorta 'Murrayana'	Mountain lodgepole pine
Pinus densiflora	Japanese red pine
Pinus densiflora 'Umbraculifera'	*Tanyosho* pine
Pinus edulis	Piñon pine
Pinus flexilis	Limber pine
Pinus halepensis	Aleppo pine
Pinus monophylla	One-needle pine
Pinus monticola	Western white pine
Pinus mugho mughus	Dwarf Mugho pine
Pinus pinea	Italian stone pine
Pinus strobus	Eastern white pine
Pinus strobus 'Nana'	Dwarf white pine
Pinus sylvestris 'Nana'	Dwarf Scotch pine
Pinus thunbergiana	Japanese black pine
Pistacia chinensis	Chinese pistachio
Platanus occidentalis	Buttonwood
Podocarpus nivalis	Alpine yew
Populus tremuloides	Quaking aspen
Potentilla fruticosa	Shrubby cinquefoil
Prunus cistena	Dwarf flowering plum

Prunus hally jollivette	Pink flowering cherry
Prunus mume	Japanese flowering apricot
Prunus serrula	Birchbark cherry
Prunus serrulata	Japanese flowering cherry
Prunus tomentosa	Nanking cherry red fruit
Prunus virginiana	Choke cherry
Pseudolarix kaempferi	Golden larch
Punica granatum 'Nana'	Dwarf pomegranate
Pyracantha 'Red Elf'	Compact firethorn
Pyrus kawakamii	Evergreen pear
Pyrus salicifolia 'Pendula'	Willowleaf pear
Quercus dumosa	California scrub oak
Quercus ilex	Holly oak
Quercus myrsinifolia	Japanese evergreen oak

Picea pungens glauca nana, *Dwarf Colorado Blue spruce.*

Pinus contorta *"Spaans dwarf," Lodgepole pine.*

Pinus contorta globosa, *Lodgepole pine.*

Pinus parviflora glauca, *Japanese White pine.*

Pinus densiflora *"Tanyosho Compacta,"* *Umbrella pine.*

Pinus strobus *"Griegs,"* *White pine.*

Pinus strobus nana, *Dwarf White pine*.

Pinus mugho mughue, *Dwarf Mugho pine*.

Pinus strobus *"nana," Dwarf Eastern White pine*.

Pinus strobus pendula, *Weeping White pine*.

Quercus phellos	Willowleaf oak
Quercus suber	Cork oak
Quercus vacciniifolia	Huckleberry oak
Rhododendron 'Blue Diamond'	Lavender
Rhododendron 'Bow Bells'	Pink
Rhododendron 'Ginny Gee'	Pink to white
Rhododendron 'Hotel'	Yellow
Rhododendron kiusianum	
Rhododendron 'Mucronulatum'	Deciduous purple
Rhododendron 'Nancy Evans'	Orange
Rhododendron satsuki azaleas	Many colors
Rhododendron 'Trilby'	Red

Pinus thunbergiana *"Yatsubusa," Dwarf Black pine*.

Rhododendron kurume azaleas	Many colors
Rhododendron 'Mucronulatum'	Deciduous purple
Rhododendron 'Nancy Evans'	Orange
Rhododendron satsuki azaleas	Many colors
Rhododendron 'Trilby'	Red
Rhodohypoxis baurii	Dwarf bulbs
Salix purpurea 'Nana'	Dwarf Alaskan blue willow
Salix sachalinensis 'Setsuka'	*Setsuka* willow
Schefflera arboricola	Hawaiian elf schefflera
Serissa foetida	Chinese snow rose
Sorbus reducta	Dwarf ash
Sorbus tianshanica	Turkestan mountain ash
Styrax japonicus	Japanese snowbell tree
Syringa koreana	Korean lilac
Taxodium distichum	Bald cypress
Taxodium mucronatum	Montezuma cypress
Taxus cuspidata 'Nana'	Dwarf Japanese yew
Taxus media 'Brownii'	Brown's yew
Thuja occidentalis 'Little Giant'	Little giant arborvitae
Thuja occidentalis 'Nana'	Dwarf arborvitae
Tilia cordata	Little leaf linden
Tsuga canadensis 'Redula'	Weeping hemlock
Ulmus parvifolia	Chinese elm
Ulmus parvifolia 'Hokkaido'	*Hokkaido* elm
Ulmus parvifolia 'Seiju'	*Seiju* elm

Ulmus parvifolia *"Seiju,"* Seiju *elm.*

Tsuga Canadensis *"Everet Golden,"* Canadian hemlock.

Tsuga Canadensis *"Redula,"* Weeping hemlock

Wisteria floribunda	Japanese wisteria
Wisteria sinensis	Chinese wisteria
Zelkova serrata	Sawleaf Zelkova
Ziziphus jujuba	Chinese date tree

THE ART OF SAIKEI

Bonsai Glossary

Accompaniment plantings A landscape in nature with plants and trees that would normally grow in the same environment; particular attention paid to compatible scale, color, variety, species

Acerifolius Maple-like leaf form

Adpressus Pressing against; hugging plant form

Air-layering The process in which roots are developed on a stem or branch which is above the ground

Albus White color

Altus Tall plant form

Angustifolius Narrow leaf form

Apex The culminating extension of the trunk

Aquifolius Spiny leaf form

Arboreus Tree-like plant form

Argenteus Silvery color

Armatus Armed

Aureus Golden color

Australis Of Australia

Azureus Azure, sky-blue color

Baccatus Berried or berry-like

Ball shape *Tama-zukuri*; in the shape of a ball

Bankan Coiled style; a spiralled trunk

Barbatus Barbed or bearded

Bilobate Divided into two lobes, as of a leaf

Bipinnate Doubly pinnate, as of a leaf consisting of a central axis and lateral axes to which leaflets are attached

Bolt The growth of a plant too quickly to flowering at the expense of good overall development

Bonkei A landscape created with sand, gravel, boats, huts, figurines, and lanterns in a large, flat tray-shaped pot with no living plants

Bonseki A landscape created with mini figurines, nonliving foliage, and the appearance of water created with a mirror

Borealis Of the north

Bract Leaf-like appendage at the base of a flower; sometimes brightly colored as in poinsettia

Broadleaf Foliage which is not a needle shape or scale-like

Broom style *Hoki-dachi, Hoki-zukuri, Hokidachi*; a style intended to resemble the shape of a broom; best suited to twiggy deciduous trees

Bulb style *Shitakusa*; perennials

Bunjin Bunjinji Literati style; free-form style that is unexplainable, personal; but knowledgeable, and respective of rules of style, design, and growth

Buxifolius Leaves like boxwood

Caesius Blue-grey color

Cambium A thin formative layer consisting of xylem and phloem in all woody plants that gives rise to new cells, is responsible for secondary growth, and transmits nutrients

Campanulatus Bell- or cup-shaped

Campestris Of the field or plains

Canadensis Of Canada

Canariensis Of the Canary Islands

Candidus Pure white color; shiny

Candle-flame shape *Rosoku-zukuri*; in the shape of a candle flame; *arborvitae*, for example

Canus Ashy grey color

Capensis Of the Cape of Good Hope

Capitatus Head-like

Carneus "Flesh"-colored, pinkish beige

Catkin String of single-sex flowers, without petals, often pendulous; found on trees such as alder, birch, and willow

Cereus Waxy

Chilensis Of Chile

Chinensis Of China

Chlorosis A diseased condition in plants characterized by yellowing; frequently caused by a lack of iron

Chokkan Formal upright style; straight, vertical trunk

Ciliaris Fringed

Citrinus Yellow color

Clustered style *Tsukami-yose*; clustered group with multiple trunks springing from one tree

Coccineus Scarlet color

Coeruleus Dark blue color

Coiled style *Bankan*; a spiralled trunk

Compactus Compact, dense plant shape

Compound leaf A leaf consisting of two or more leaflets

Concolor One color

Cone Fruit of a conifer consisting of wood scales enclosing naked multiple ovules or seeds

Confertus Crowded, pressed-together plant shape

Conifer Cone-bearing plant; may be deciduous

Cordatus Cordate; heart-shaped

Cornutus Horned

Crassus Thick, fleshy

Croceus Yellow color

Cruentus Bloody color

Culm The hollow-jointed stems of grasses, especially bamboo

Cultivar Cultivated variety; see *subspecies* and *variety*

Cultural dwarf Manipulation of growth characteristics which results in dwarfing

Cutting Any plant fragment cut off for the purpose of rooting a new plant

Damping off Fungus disease usually attacking cuttings or seedlings

Deciduous Referring to plants that drop their leaves or needles at the end of the growing season

Decumbens Lying-down plant shape

Decurrens Running down the stem

Defoliate The early removal of leaves; a common artificial technique in bonsai training

-dendron Tree

Dentate Sharply toothed leaf margins

Depressus Pressed-down plant shape

Desiccate To dry up or cause to dry up

Dieback A progressive plant condition characterized by stem failure, starting from the tips of leaves and branches. Could be disease, insect, or environmental damage

Discolor Two colors; separate colors

Dissected Usually a highly intricate natural cutting of a leaf, as in *Acer palmatum dissectum*, also called laceleaf

Diversi Varying

Double-trunk style *Sokan*; two trunks attached to each other in the bottom quarter of the tree; the larger of the two trunks is displayed slightly forward of the smaller

Driftwood style *Sarimiki, Sharimiki*; large areas of dead wood; desert, beach, or high-altitude appearance

Drip line A circle directly under a tree that corresponds to where water drips on the ground, usually just inside the tips of the lower branches

Earth layering Creating roots on a stem or branch by burying a section in the ground

Edulis Edible

Elegans Elegant; slender, willowy plant shape

Elongated style *Goza-kake*; exaggerated first branch balanced by a special wide pot; sometimes found over water

Epiphyte A plant that grows on another for support; not to be confused with parasite

Exposed-root style *Ne-agari*; air space under roots that suggests erosion

Eye An undeveloped growth bud

Fallen-cone style *Yama-yori*; hundred-tree style; hundreds of sprouts from one vicinity

Fastigiatus Branches erect and close together

Five-tree style *Gohon-yose*; a group planting of five trees

Floridus Free-flowering

Formal Regular, rigid, and geometric, as in formal upright design

Formal cascade style *Kengai*; first branch extends below the bottom edge of the pot; pot sits on a stand

Formal upright style *Chokkan*; straight, vertical trunk

Fruticosus Shrubby

Fukunigashi Windswept style; the slant of the tree indicates wind direction, as though the tree were growing on a mountain or near a beach; slant may be extreme or gentle

Fulgens Shiny

Genetic dwarf Small size and other characteristics are genetically determined

Genus A classification of related plants; the first word in a botanical name

Glaucus Covered with grey bloom

Gohon-yose Five-tree style; a group planting of five trees

Goza-kake Elongated style; exaggerated first branch balanced by a special wide pot; sometimes found over water

Gracilis Slender, thin, small plant shape

Grandis Large, showy plant shape

Grass plantings *Kusamomo*, including bamboo

Group-planting style *Yose-uye, Yose-ue*; more than nine trees or any larger prime number; a grove or group planting rather than a forest

Han-kengai Semi-cascade style; foliage of first branch must extend below the top edge of the pot. *Dai-kengai*: vertical cascade; *Gaito-kengai*: mountaintop cascade; *Taki-kengai*: waterfall cascade; *Ito-kengai*: string cascade; *Takan-kengai*: two-trunk cascade

Harden off The progressive

adaptation of a tender plant to the full brunt of harsh outdoor conditions

Hardy   A plant that can resist cold; usually expressed as hardy to $-15°F$ ($-26°C$), for example

Heavy soil   A term which is commonly used to describe clay or compacted soils

Herbaceous   Nonwoody

Hokidachi, Hoki-dachi, Hoki-zukuri   Broom style; a style intended to resemble the shape of a broom; best suited to twiggy deciduous trees

Hollow-trunk style   *Sabakan*; as the heartwood rots away in some species, a hollowed-out trunk is formed; live oak, coast redwood

Honeydew   Any secretion caused by sucking insects on a plant, usually attracting ants

Hortensis   Of gardens

Humilis   Low, small, humble plant form

Humisusis   Sprawling plant form

Humus   The late stages of rotting organic material

Hundred-tree style   *Yama-yori*, fallen-cone style; hundreds of sprouts from one vicinity

Hybrid   Plant created by crossing two species of the same genus or two varieties of the same species

-ifer, -iferus   Bearing or having

Ikadabuki   Raft style; single tree on its side with branches trained upright as though they were all individual trees; visually creates a forest

Ilicifolius   Holly-like leaves

Impressus   Impressed upon

Incanus   Grey color

Informal upright style   *Moyogi,*

Tachiki; curving upright trunk; apex is over rootage

Internode   A section of a stem between two successive nodes

Insularis   Of the island

Ishizuke, Ishitsuke, or Ishitzuki   Rocky-garden style characterized by entire tree planted on a rock, but no soil in the pot; possibly water, sand, or bare glaze in the bottom of the pot

Jin   The dead apex of a tree, usually found only on hardwood trees; literally means "God" and is symbolic of the Supreme Being's influence on nature

Kabudachi   Sprout style, *Miyama-kirishima*; characterized by sprouts which have developed on an old stump, a section of fallen tree, or part of a rotten log; sprouts arranged like flowers to contrast new life with old tree

Kasa-zukuri   Umbrella shape; in the shape of an umbrella

Kengai   Formal cascade style; first branch extends below the bottom edge of the pot; pot sits on a stand

Knobby-trunk style   *Kobukan*; healed-over sprouts; often caused by stress in nature

Kusamomo   Grass plantings, including bamboo

Kyuhon-yose   Nine-trunk style; a group planting of nine trees

Laciniatus   Fringed or with torn edges

Laevigatus   Smooth

Lanceolate   Lance-shaped

Lateral   Positioned at the side; an extension of a branch or a shoot

Lath   Usually refers to a series of wooden boards erected above plants to provide artificial shade

Laurifolius   Laurel-like leaves

Leaching   The removal of substances from the soil by excess watering

Leader   The dominant upward single central growth of a plant

Leaf mould   Partially decomposed leaves; not yet humus

Leaf scar   The slight indentation left on a twig that remains after a leaf stalk is removed

Leaflet   Divisions of a leaf, either palmate (fan-shaped) or pinnate (feather-shaped)

Legume   Pod or seed vessel of the pea family, splitting lengthwise to release seeds

Light soil   Commonly referred to as sandy soil; more precisely, well-aerated soil

Linear   Long and narrow, with parallel sides

Literati style   See *Bunjin, Bunjinji*

Littoralis   Of the seashore

Lobatus   Lobed; projection or division of a leaf or petal

Luteus   Reddish yellow color

Maculatus   Spotted

Matsu-zukuri   Pine-tree shape; in the shape of a pine tree; may also be used for deciduous trees

Meristem   A formative plant tissue usually made up of small cells capable of dividing indefinitely and giving rise to similar cells or to cells that differentiate to produce the definitive tissues and organs

Miyama-kirishima   Sprout style, *Kabudachi*; characterized by sprouts which have developed on an old stump, a section of fallen tree, or part of a rotten log; sprouts arranged like flowers to contrast new life with old tree

Mollis   Soft, soft and hairy

Montanus   Of the mountains

Moyogi   *Tachiki*, informal upright style; curving upright trunk; apex is over rootage

Mucronatus   Pointed; terminating in a point

Mulch   A loose, organic covering over soil or to describe the process of applying such a layer

Nanahon-yose   Seven-trunk style; a group planting of seven trees

Nanus   Dwarf

Natural dwarf   A plant which is dwarfed by the forces of nature

Natural style   *Yomayori, Yomayose*; natural, informal grouping

Ne-agari   Exposed-root style; air space under roots that suggests erosion

Nejikan   Twisted style; trunk spirals upwards with growth

Netsunari   Root-connected style; trees sprout from long surface roots of more than one rootstock; occurs naturally in willow, quince, Chinese raintree, vine maple, wild cherry

Nine-trunk style   *Kyuhon-yose*; a group planting of nine trees

Node   Joints occurring at intervals along the stem of a plant from which a leaf or bud develops

Nutans   Nodding, swaying

Obtusus   Blunt or flattened

Octopus style   *Tako-zukuri, Takozukuri*; overexaggeration of informal upright style with many zigs and zags, including rootage and branches

Officinalis   Medicinal

-oides   Like or resembling

Opposite   Leaf arrangements in pairs along an axis, one opposite the other

Organic matter   Any material that was alive at some point; for example, peat, bark, and manure

Ovate   Egg-shaped, with the larger part towards the base

Palmate   With leaflets or lobes radiating like outstretched fingers from a central point

Parasite   A plant growing on another and using up nutrients from the host plant

Parvifolius   Small leaves

Patens   Open, spreading

Peeled-bark style   *Sharikan*; damage to bark as the result of lightning or other trauma; not driftwood

P'en Tsai   The Chinese word for bonsai, an art form which predates the Japanese art

Perennial   A nonwoody plant that lives for three years or more

Perlite   Natural minerals expanded by heat to form a light, porous granule for use in propagating or lightening soils

Petiole   Leaf stalk

Phloem   A complex tissue in the vascular system of higher plants consisting mainly of sieve tubes and elongated cells. Its fibres function in translocation, support, and storage

Pinching back   Nipping of tips of branches by hand

Pine-tree shape   *Matsu-zukuri*; in the shape of a pine tree; may also be used for deciduous trees

Pinnate, pinnatus   A compound leaf with leaflets, usually paired on either side of the stalk like a feather

Plenus   Double, full

Plumosus   Feathery

Populifolius   Poplar-like leaves

Praecox   Precocious

Procumbens   Trailing plant shape

Prostratus   Prostrate plant shape

Pumilus   Dwarfish, small plant shape

Pungens   Piercing

Purpureus   Purple color

Radicans   Rooting, especially along the stem

Raft style   *Ikadabuki*; single tree on its side with branches trained upright as though they were all individual trees; visually creates a forest

Repens, reptans   Creeping plant shape

Reticulatus   Net-veined

Retusus   Notched at blunt apex

Rhizome   Modified stem which develops horizontally underground

Riparius   Of river banks

Rivalis, rivularis   Of brooks

Rock-garden style   See *Ishizuke, Ishitsuke, Ishitzuki*

Root-connected style   *Netsunari*; trees sprout from long surface roots of more than one rootstock; occurs naturally in willow, quince, Chinese raintree, vine maple, wild cherry

Root-over-rock style   *Sekijoju*; tree roots placed over and trained to grow on one or more rocks; trees may be planted immediately in this manner or developed gradually

Rootstock   Part of a grafted plant which supplies the roots; same as understock

Roso-zukuri   Candle-flame shape; in the shape of a candle flame; *arborvitae*

Rubens, ruber   Red, ruddy color

Rufus Ruddy color

Rugosus Wrinkled, rough

Sabakan See Hollow-trunk style

Sabamiki, Shaba-miki A bonsai design element that copies natural hollowing and decay of the trunks of hardwood trees; may include the characteristic twisting of the juniper species, the hollowing-out of oak, or the vertical stripping of the trunk as branches die off as in timberline trees

Saccharatus Sweet, sugary

Sagittalis Arrow-like

Saikei A "living landscape" of trees planted on rocks, with streams, cliffs, valleys, and caves; contained in a large, flat tray-shaped pot—rock-grown style; multiple trees; multiple rocks; multiple trees and rocks; multiple pots

Saikei forest planting Characterized by particular emphasis placed upon a detail, such as trunks, foliage, number of trees, or landscape feature

Saikei one tree Placement of one tree next to other elements, such as rock(s), mountain, stream, bush, ridge, mountaintop, cave, natural bridge, etc.

Saikei two tree Characterized by harmony, balance, interest, and stability of trees and landscape features; similarities in shape, front and back, direction, profile, spacing, position, interval. Also, three-tree, five-tree, group planting

Salicifolius Willow-like leaves

Sambon-yose Three-tree style; relationship between height, width, branches, and depth is symbolic of sun, moon, and earth; or heaven, earth, and man; or father, mother, and child

Saramiki *Sharimiki*, driftwood style; large areas of dead wood; desert, beach, or high-altitude appearance

Saxatilis Inhabiting rocks

Scabrus Rough-feeling

Scandens Climbing plant shape

Scoparius Broom-like

Sekijoju Root over rock; tree roots placed over and trained to grow on one or more rocks; trees may be planted immediately in this manner or developed gradually

Semi-cascade style See *Han-kengai*; foliage of first branch must extend below top edge of the pot

Seven-trunk style *Nanahon-yose*; a group of planting of seven trees

Shakan Slanting style; straight or curved trunk; slant is not forward or backwards; apex is not over roots. *Sho-shakan*: minimum slant; *Chu-shakan*: medium slant; *Dai-shakan*: maximum slant

Shari A dead branch or fragment of a dead branch found on hardwood species; found as a horizontal design motif

Sharikan Peeled-bark style; damage to bark as the result of lightning or other trauma; not driftwood

Sharimiki *Saramiki*, driftwood style; large areas of dead wood; desert, beach, or high-altitude appearance

Shidare-zukuri Weeping style; fashioned after the weeping willow tree

Shitakusa Bulb style; perennials

Slanting style *Shakan*; straight or curved trunk; slant is not forward or backwards; apex is not over roots

Soju, So-ju Two-tree style; relationship between tree heights, widths, lowest branches creates illusion of tree in the distance

Sokan Double-trunk style; two trunks, preferably in the bottom quarter of the tree and one in front of the other

Species The word in a botanical name following the genus

Sphagnum Bog mosses that are collected as a source of organic soil amendment

Split-trunk style *Sabamiki*; the trunk of the tree has split due to trauma; one side may be dead

Spore A simple cell for reproduction in some primitive plants, such as ferns, algae, and moss

Sport Genetic mutation

Sprout style *Miyama-kirishima*, *Kabudachi*; characterized by sprouts which have developed on an old stump, a section of fallen tree, or part of a rotten log; sprouts arranged like flowers to contrast new life with old tree

Spur Specialized short branch on a fruit tree which produces the blossom

Stomata Microscopically small openings in the epidermis of the green parts of a tree or other plant through which gases pass out of and into the plant from the air

Stratification The plant and seed requirement for certain minimum cold periods before successful seed germination or flowering

Stress Any plant condition that threatens its health, such as too much water or too little water

Subspecies The word in a botanical name following the

genus and species, expressed in lower case letters, that sometimes precedes the variety or cultivar, which, in contrast, are expressed in roman letters with an initial cap and surrounded by quotation marks

Sucker Plant growth on a grafted plant that originates on the rootstock; also improper term for watersprout on fruit trees

Suiseki A viewing rock or stone placed on a custom-made, carved and footed wooden stand. The stone is viewed from a specific perspective

Symbiotic Describes relationship between two plants in which mutual benefit is derived

Systemic Any chemical product which is transported into the sap of the plant by absorption; the pest at which it is directed is poisoned as it eats its plant "host"

Tachiki *Moyogi*, informal upright style; curving upright trunk; apex is over rootage

Takozukuri, Tako-zukuri Octopus style; overexaggeration of informal upright style with many zigs and zags, including roots and branches

Tama-zukuri Ball-shaped

Taproot A large, central root that grows fast and straight down for the purpose of reaching a deep water table

Tender Not hardy; usually genetic, but could be used to refer to plants that need to be hardened off

Thinning out Pruning to achieve a more open structure in the plant

Three-tree style *Sambon-yose*; relationship between height, width, branches, and depth is symbolic of sun, moon and earth; or heaven, earth, and man; or father, mother, and child

Top dress To add material, such as mulch or fertilizer, to the surface of the soil

Topiary The art of shaping bushes and trees into unnatural shapes, such as animals or mazes

Tosho Triple-trunk style; similar to three-trunk style except that all three trunks come from the same tree

Truss A terminal cluster of flowers, such as in the rhododendron species

Tsukami-yose Clustered style; a group style with multiple trunks springing from one tree

Twisted style *Nejikan*; trunk spirals upwards with growth

Two-tree style *Soju, So-ju*; relationship between tree heights, widths, and lowest branches creates illusion of a tree in the distance

Umbrella shape *Kasa-zukuri*; in the shape of an umbrella

Underplanting Planting a low plant under a larger one, such as a ground cover under a tall shrub

Understock See **Rootstock**

Variety Also cultivar; any capitalized name in roman letters with quotation marks around it when included in a botanical name

and usually following the genus and species—and subspecies, if included—such as *Juniperus chinensis sargentii* 'Shimpaku'

Vermiculite Heat-puffed mica, a soil-lightening amendment

Watersprout Unchecked, sudden upward growth as the result of severe pruning

Weeping style *Shidare-zukuri*; fashioned after the weeping willow tree

Wettable powder A pesticide that can be applied by first mixing with water

Whorl Three or more leaves, branches, or stems growing out from one location on a branch; best known as a problem in pine bonsai design

Windswept style *Fukunigashi*; the slant of the tree indicates wind direction, as though the tree were growing on a mountain or near a beach; slant may be extreme or gentle

Yama-yori Fallen-cone style, hundred-tree style; hundreds of sprouts from one vicinity

Yatsabusa Plant name designation simply meaning extremely dwarfed; such plant material generally makes an excellent candidate for saikei

Yomayori, Yomayose Natural style; natural informal grouping

Yose-ue, Yose-uye Group planting style; more than nine trees or any larger prime number; a grove or group planting rather than a forest

Suggested Reading List

Adams, Peter D. *The Art of Bonsai*; London: Ward Lock, 1981.

———. *Bonsai Design: Japanese Maples*; New York: Sterling Publishing Co., 1988.

———*Successful Bonsai Gardening*; London: Ward Lock, 1978.

Ainsworth, John. *The Art of Indoor Bonsai*; London: Ward Lock, 1988.

Behme, Robert Lee. *Bonsai, Saikei and Bonkei: Japanese Dwarf Trees and Tray Landscapes*; New York: W. Morrow, 1969.

Bollman, Willi E. *Kamuti: A New Way in Bonsai*; London: Faber, 1974.

Brooklyn Botanic Gardens. *Handbook on Bonsai: Special Techniques*; Brooklyn, NY, 1977.

———*Handbook on Dwarfed Potted Trees: The Bonsai of Japan*; Brooklyn, NY, 1974.

Chan, Peter. *Bonsai Masterclass*; New York: Sterling Publishing Co., 1988.

———*Create Your Own Bonsai with Everyday Garden Plants*; Vancouver, BC: Cavendish Books, Inc., 1989.

Chidamian, Claude. *Bonsai: Miniature Trees*; Princeton, NJ: Van Nostrand, 1955.

Clark, Randy T. *Outstanding American Bonsai*; Portland, OR: Timber Press, 1989.

Derderian, C. T. *Bonsai for Indoors*; Brooklyn, NY: Brooklyn Botanic Gardens, 1976.

Engel, David H. *Creating a Chinese Garden*; London: Croom Helm, 1986.

Giorgi, Gianfranco. *Guide to Bonsai*; New York: Simon and Schuster, 1990.

Gustafson, Herb L. *The Bonsai Workshop*; New York: Sterling Publishing Co., 1994.

Hall, George Frederick. *Bonsai for Americans: A Practical Guide to the Creation and Care of Miniature Potted Trees*; Garden City, NY: Doubleday, 1964.

Hirota, Jozan. *Bonkei: Tray Landscapes*; Tokyo: Kodansha International, 1970.

Ishimoto, Tatsuo. *The Art of Growing Miniature Plants and Landscapes: Japanese Bonsai and Bonkei Adapted to American Conditions*; New York: Crown Publishing, 1956.

Katayama, Teiichi. *The Mini-Bonsai Hobby*; Tokyo: Japan Publications; Distributed by Japan Publications Trading Co., 1974.

Kawamoto, Toshio. *Saikei: Living Landscapes in Miniature*; Tokyo: Kodansha International, 1967.

Kawasumi, Masakuni. *Bonsai with American Trees*; Tokyo: Kodansha International, 1975.

Koide, Nobukichi, Saburo Kato, and Fusza Takeyama. *The Masters Book of Bonsai*; Tokyo: Kodansha International, 1967.

Larkin, H. J. *Bonsai for Beginners: The Art of Growing Miniature Trees*; New York, NY: Arco Publishing Co., 1969.

Lesniewicz, Paul. *Bonsai: The Complete Guide to Art and Technique*; Dorset, England: Blandford Press, 1984.

———*Indoor Bonsai*; Dorset, England: Blandford Press, 1985.

———*The World of Bonsai*; New York: Sterling Publishing Co., 1990.

Lifang, Chen. *The Garden Art of China*; Portland, OR: Timber Press, 1986.

Murata, Kenji. *Practical Bonsai for Beginners*; Tokyo: Japan Publications Trading Co., 1964.

Murata, Kyuzo. *Bonsai, Miniature Potted Trees*; Tokyo: Shufunotomo Co., Ltd., 1964.

———*Introductory Bonsai and the Care and Use of Bonsai Tools*; Tokyo: Japan Publications, 1971.

Naka, John Yoshio. *Bonsai Techniques*; Santa Monica, CA: Dennis-Landman Publishers, 1975.

————and others. *Bonsai Techniques for Satsuki*; Ota Bonsai Nursery, 1979.

Nakamura, Zeko. *Bonsai Miniatures: Quick and Easy*; Tokyo: Shufunotomo Co., Ltd., 1973.

Nippon Bonsai Association. *Classic Bonsai of Japan*; translated by Jon Bestor; New York: Kodansha International/USA, 1989.

Ohashi, Haruzo. *Japanese Courtyard Gardens*; Tokyo: Graphic-Sha Publishing, 1988.

Perl, Philip. *Miniatures and Bonsai*; Alexandria, VA: Time-Life Books, 1979.

Pike, David. *Bonsai, Step by Step to Growing Success*; Ramsbury, England: The Crowood Press, 1989.

Roger, Alan. *Bonsai*; London: The Royal Horticultural Society; 1989.

Samson, Isabelle and Remy. *The Creative Art of Bonsai*; London: Ward Lock, Ltd., 1986.

Stewart, Christine. *Bonsai*; London: Orbis, 1981.

Stowell, Jerald P. *The Beginner's Guide to American Bonsai*; Tokyo: Kodansha International, 1978.

———— *Bonsai, Indoors and Out: How to Grow Decorative Trees from Hardy and Tender Plants*; Princeton, NJ: Van Nostrand, 1966.

Sunset Books and Magazines. *Bonsai: Culture and Care of Miniature Trees*; Menlo Park, CA: Lane Publishing Co., 1976.

Valavanis, William N. *Bonsai Creation and Design Using Propagation Techniques*; Atlanta, GA: Symmes Systems, 1975.

————*The Japanese Five-Needled Pine: Nature, Gardens, Bonsai Taxonomy*; Atlanta, GA: Symmes Systems, 1976.

Van Gelderen, D. M., and J. R. P. Van Hoey Smith. *Conifers*; Portland, OR: Timber Press, 1986.

Vertrees, J. D. *Japanese Maples*; Portland, OR: Timber Press, 1987.

Webber, Leonard. *Bonsai for the Home and Garden*; North Ryde, NSW, Australia: Agus and Robertson/Salem House, 1985.

Yashiroda, Kan. *Bonsai, Japanese Miniature Trees: Their Style, Cultivation and Training*; Newton, MA: C. T. Branford Co., 1960.

Yonhua, Ho. *Chinese Penjing, Miniature Trees and Landscapes*; Portland, OR: Timber Press, 1987.

Yoshimura, Yuji. *The Japanese Art of Miniature Trees and Landscapes: Their Creation, Care and Enjoyment*; Rutland, VA: C. E. Tuttle, 1957.

Index

A

Acer burgerianum, 110
Acer palmatum, 30–31
Acer rubrum, 115
Aesthetics, 76–78
Ancient gorgo, 131–133
Animal stone, 84–87
Annual care. *See* Care
Aphids, 162–163
Arborvitae, 32, 131
Artist brushes, 57

B

Background, 36–37
Balance, 59–61
Basalt, 23
Beach rock, 25
Beach sand, 26
Beginners, 20
Bench, growing, 69
Big valley, 102
Bonkei, 17, 18
Bonsai
    related art forms, 18–20
    soil. *See* Soil, bonsai
    vs. saikei, 17
Bonseki, 18
Branch splitter, 65
Brookside, 110–114
Brushes, 66–67
Bunjin style, 20

C

Cactus, 30, 126
Canyon, water-formed, 102
Care, 140
    diseases and, 163–164

fertilizing, 162
insects, 162–163
mystery problems and, 164
pruning, 150
replacing planting, 156–157
repotting, 151–155
summer, 158–159
watering, 160–162
winter, 158–159
Cascade style, 109
Cast aluminum scoops, 67–68
Chamaecyparis thyoides, 32
Chamaecyparis thyoides andelyensis, 32
Chamaecyparis thyoides andelyensis conica, 131
Chinese elm, 20, 42
Chinese P'en Jing. *See* P'en Jing
Chinzan azaleas, 127–130
Chopsticks, 65–66
Cleaning, for repotting, 152–153
Coastal steam, 102–103
Color
    depth and, 48–51
    harmony and, 55
    of pots, 18–19
Composition, development, 101–103
Compressed-air sprayer, compact, 69
Concave cutter, 65
Consistency, 55–59
Containers, 20–22, 70–71
    color, harmony and, 55
    making, 22
    preparing for repotting, 154–155
    removal from, 152
    scale of, 62
    sizes, 20–22, 33
    trunk size and, 21–22
Copper-clad aluminum wire, 68
Copper wire, 68

Cork bark elm, 29, 42
Cosmetics brush, 67
Creation
    ancient gorge, 131–133
    brookside and, 110–114
    Chinese P'en Jing, 122–125
    desert arroyo, 126–127
    natural bridge, 118–121
    nature's hardships and, 110
    old growth, 115
    Olduvai gorge, 140–141
    outcropping, 109–110
    overlooking the stream, 110
    rocky plateau, 105–108
    root-over-rock maple, 139
    sandstone shoreline, 134–138
    shelter cave, 115
    stream-side grove, 115
    timberline, 142–147
    unicorn garden, 127–130
Curved stone, 92

D

Dai-shakan, 105
Depth, 36–37
    color and, 48–51
    details and, 41–45
    rock placement and, 40–41
    tree placement and, 37–39
Desert arroyo, 126–127
Details, depth and, 41–45
Devil's post pile, 27
Diseases, 163–164
Disposable foam-type brush, 66
Distant mountain stone, 89–90

E

Elm varieties, 29
Euphorbia, 30
"Executive Sandbox," 93

The Author

Herb Gustafson has been growing and studying plants for almost 40 years. He first began collecting miniature plants as a schoolboy, years before he heard the word *bonsai*, arranging them on his windowsill in small containers. After an early career as a widely travelled (82 countries) and published primatologist and nature photographer, he settled down to his first love, as owner of a mail-order bonsai and saikei nursery. He teaches at local colleges where his adult, continuing education students have been a major influence on his writing about bonsai and saikei. Herb received a grant in the early 1970s to study Japanese macaque monkeys that took him to Tokyo. There his standing as an already published author of a book on bonsai lead to his acceptance at the Nippon Bonsai Saikei Institute. He remained in Japan for two years, also studying privately with some of the masters at bonsai nurseries in Omiya, Japan's "bonsai village." Over the years his teachers have included John Naka, T'ai Chi Katayama, Toshio Kawamoto, Zeko Nakamura, Kenji Murata, and Wu Yee Sun. Herb is affiliated with the Japan Bonsai Association, the American Bonsai Society, and Bonsai Clubs International. His previous works include *The Bonsai Workshop* published in 1994 (Sterling Publishing Co., Inc.). Herb and his wife, Susan, live in Eugene, Oregon.